D0811959

TIMECHANGES

GEOFFREY TREASE

12.95

8-29-85

86-0069

600
Tre

WARWICK PRESS

Above left: The Great Vault at King's College, Cambridge, built in the mid-15th century.

Above right: Early 20th-century French advertisement for various forms of wheeled transport.

Bottom right: Röntgen demonstrating his new invention – X-rays. He discovered that radiation produced by a strong electrical discharge onto a cathode in a vacuum passed through paper, wood and flesh but not metal or bone. Röntgen called them 'X' meaning unknown.

ACKNOWLEDGEMENTS

Front and back covers top left John Cannon, top centre Mary Evans Picture Library, top right British Airways, bottom left Science Museum, London, bottom centre J. Allan Cash, bottom right Sonia Halliday; 6 right National Motor Museum; 7 The BBC Hulton Picture Library; 8 centre Cambridge University Museum of Archaeology and Anthropology, bottom Sonia Halliday; 9 top Science Museum, London, bottom The BBC Hulton Picture Library; 10 centre left British Library; 11 bottom ZEFA; 12 centre left The BBC Hulton Picture Library, centre right Mansell Collection, bottom right I.T.N.; 13 centre left School of Slavonic and East European Studies, University of London, centre right The BBC Hulton Picture Library, bottom Health Education Council; 15 top Ford Motor Co; 17 ZEFA; 18 bottom The BBC Hulton Picture Library/Bettman Archives; 19 top right Popperfoto, centre right N.A.S.A., bottom right British Aerospace; 20 centre right Mary Evans Picture Library, bottom left Rolls Royce, bottom right The BBC Hulton Picture Library; 21 centre The BBC Hulton Picture Library, bottom ZEFA; 22 The BBC Hulton Picture Library/Bettman Archives; 23 top Barry Searle/S. Halliday Photos, centre Mansell Collection, bottom left Mary Evans Picture Library, bottom right F.H.C. Birch/S. Halliday Photos; 24 top Naval Photo Center, Washington; 25 top Royal Ordnance Factories; 27 top Yorkshire and Humberside Tourist Board; 28 bottom Frank Spooner; 20 top and bottom left Henry Grant, bottom right David redfern; 30 bottom left Georgia Dept Community Development, bottom centre Hoover Ltd; 31 top Singer Co U.K. Ltd, bottom Dave Collins; 33 top David Shilling; 34 National Gallery, London; 35 centre Victoria and Albert Museum; 36 bottom left The Bridgeman Art Library, bottom right Atari; 37 George Beal; 39 top Colorsport, centre right Don Morley, bottom right Colorsport; 40 bottom ZEFA; 42 top Mary Evans Picture Library; 44 top left British Museum, top right National Museum, Greece, centre top left and centre top right National Gallery, London, centre bottom left Fitzwilliam Museum, centre bottom right Scala, bottom National Gallery, London; 45 top left British Museum, top centre left Fitzwilliam Museum, top centre right Scala, top right, centre left and centre National Gallery, London, centre right Scala, bottom left John Webb, bottom centre Bridgeman Art Library, bottom right Tate Gallery, London; 46 Sonia Halliday; 47 Kodak Museum; 48 top Pat Morris, bottom right The BBC Hulton Picture Library; 49 left Mansell Collection; 51 bottom centre right ZEFA; 52 top ZEFA, bottom Scala; 54 top Sonia Halliday/Laura Lushington; 55 left Lucinda Lambton/ARCAID; 56 top Victoria and Albert Museum; 57 top Museum of Modern Art, New York, Gift of Herbert Bayer; 59 top Tower Housewares, bottom Richard Bryant; 61 centre J. Allan Cash; 62 top Richard Bryant; 63 top Richard Bryant; 65 top I.B.M.; 67 top Science Museum, London, bottom left Fotomas; 69 top Michael Holford, bottom Zeiss; 70 bottom left Mary Evans Picture Library; 71 bottom right St Mary's Hospital Medical School; 72 top Paul Brierley; 74 top Fred Spencer, bottom International Tin Research Institute; 79 bottom left Sonia Halliday; 80 Sonia Halliday; 83 top Courtaulds; 84 bottom left ZEFA; 85 bottom right Argonne National Laboratory; 87 bottom Renault; 88 bottom left Frank Spooner, bottom right Popperfoto; 90 top ZEFA; 91 top Mansell Collection;

Editorial

Author
Geoffrey Trease

Editor
Adrian Sington

Designer
Ben White

Published 1985 by Warwick Press,
387 Park Avenue South, New York, New York 10016.
First published in Great Britain by
Kingfisher Books Ltd., 1985.
Copyright © Grisewood & Dempsey Ltd. 1985.

Printed in Italy by Vallardi Industrie Grafiche, Milan.

6 5 4 3 2 1 All rights reserved

Library of Congress Catalog Card No. 84-51394
ISBN 0-531-09230-5

Contents

A World of Change — 8

PASSING THE WORD
Writing it Down — 10
Spreading the News — 12

TRAVEL AND TRANSPORT
Highway and Railway — 14
All Aboard — 16
The Conquest of the Air — 18
Seeing the World — 20

WAR AND ARMAMENTS
The Causes of War — 22
The Warrior and his Weapons — 24
The Art of Self-Defence — 26

CLOTHES AND FASHION
Fashion — 28
Clothes — 30
Top and Toe — 32
For Appearance's Sake — 34

LEISURE AND PLEASURE
Toys and Games — 36
Sport — 38
The Theatre — 40
From Pipe to Pop — 42
Magic of Painting — 44

The Hand of the Craftsman — 46
Indulgences — 48

HOME, SWEET HOME
Looking at Houses — 50
Walking In — 52
Lighting — 54
Upstairs and Downstairs — 56
The Kitchen — 58
Home Comforts — 60
The Bathroom — 62

DISCOVERING OUR WORLD
Counting and Calculating — 64
The Nature of Things — 66
Mapping the Unknown — 68
Medicine — 70

MAN AT WORK
Hunters and Herdsmen — 74
Seed and Harvest — 76
Materials, Methods and Men — 78
Projects and Plans — 80
The Industrial Revolution — 82

LIVING IN SOCIETY
Learning to Behave — 88
Money Matters — 90
Index — 92

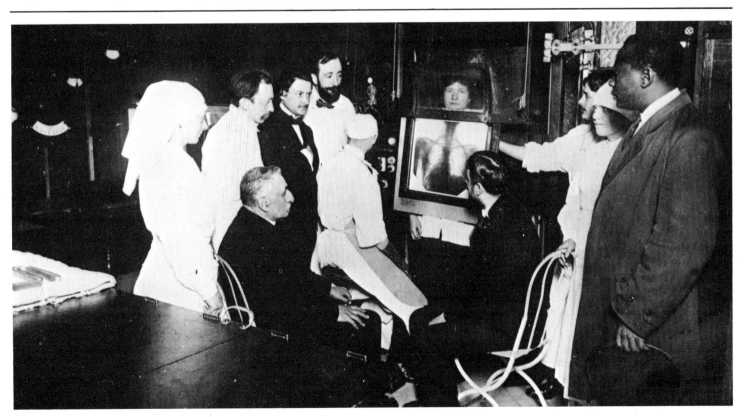

A World of Change

Do you get bored when older people go on and on, moaning about how 'times have changed'? 'Things used to be so cheap,' they say. Or, 'Things were properly made, then.' Or, 'The young knew how to behave.'

You may have heard such remarks so often that your mind automatically switches off. I know how I felt myself when my elders kept up this constant lament. That was during World War I (1914–1918) and just afterwards. Whatever else changes, such grumbling is always much the same. Greek comedians were cracking jokes about it in 400 BC.

My father kept a coin in his waistcoat pocket. Sometimes he pulled it out and let its gold flash in the light. It really *was* gold, a sovereign, with St George on one side killing the dragon. It was the only sovereign I ever handled. The government had called in all the gold when the war broke out, and for each sovereign people were given a paper one-pound note instead. My father must have broken the law by keeping this one coin for luck. This, to people of his age, was real money, not those grubby bits of paper. But they had to get used to the currency notes, for we have never had gold in our pockets again.

Many older people hate change, mainly because they feel more at ease with what they are used to. Younger people are much more ready for something new. They find it interesting and exciting. But whether we like or dislike change makes little difference, because it happens in any case, all the time.

The change may also make a considerable difference, even alter our lives. It is fascinating to see how sometimes an idea, a casual discovery, an improvement in some homely everyday article or process, can transform the future of millions, or even of all mankind.

A simple item of equipment, the stirrup, once cost the lives of an emperor and 40,000 soldiers. Some mould in a saucer has *saved* countless lives because it led to the discovery of penicillin. This book is about such changes and how they have formed the world in which we now live.

Changes are of various types. It may help to indicate some, and the words we use to describe them.

1. Technical, or technological: ways of doing work with tools or machinery, and not only in industry but in farming, medicine and so on. Anything from a vacuum cleaner to a microchip involves such changes.

2. Economic: changes to do with money and business, and so perhaps affecting pay-packets and unemployment.

3. Social: changes in the everyday life and habits of 'society'—the community, that is, or one section of it.

4. Cultural: concerned with books, plays, music, art and so on.

5. Political: either violent changes like the French Revolution or peaceful ones, like a new law to give votes to women as well as men.

Some changes may fall under several of these headings—a technical invention may go on to cause economic and social changes too. The railway certainly did. And not every 'revolution' is political—the word means only a sudden, drastic change in some field of activity. We speak of 'the Industrial Revolution' in the 18th and 19th centuries.

Certain countries at certain times have seen the start of a

▲ A contrast in cutting methods. Top: This bull's head can-opener appeared in the 1860s. Before this, tin cans which had been invented in 1811 were opened with a hammer and chisel. Above: An Australian aborigine's spearhead used for hunting, made in the Stone Age manner but out of modern bottle glass.

▼ Though there is little wind to propel this Egyptian *felucca*, its triangular lateen sail allows it to sail almost into the wind. Until its invention sails had been square, which meant that they were only effective when the wind was astern (from behind) or abeam (from the side). With the invention of the lateen sail a boat could sail into the wind by altering the position of the sail. On a river this was especially useful: boats could now sail in both directions, whereas previously they had had to row one way or wait for the wind to change.

▲ The first lawn mower is a surprisingly modern-looking machine. Yet it was patented by an English engineer in 1830. It was described then as 'a machine for cropping or shearing the vegetable surfaces of lawns, grass plots and pleasure grounds'. Budding used a rotating cutter which operated against a fixed bar. The rotating bar used the principle of Archimedes' screw, spinning the mown grass forward into a flat tray fixed to the front of the machine. The heavy roller smoothed down the mown lawn behind the machine. Before this invention, lawns were cut by horses with padded hooves pulling a cutting machine.

▼ Emily Davidson throwing herself under the King's horse at the 1913 Derby in her attempt to bring publicity to the subject of a woman's right to vote. In the same year Emily Pankhurst was put in prison for inciting persons to place explosives in Lloyd George's house. Women over 30 got the vote in 1918, reduced to 21 in 1928.

particularly large number of changes. So, as they crop up on page after page, it is useful to note their names and where they are.

Civilization began in fertile valleys where crops grew easily. The *Sumerians*, in about 3000 BC between the twin rivers Tigris and Euphrates, in Mesopotamia (now Iraq), were followed in the same region by the *Babylonians* and *Assyrians*. There were the *Egyptians* at about the same time in the Nile valley. Slightly later, on the Yellow River, the *Chinese* began their wonderful and quite separate civilization. In what is now Pakistan, in the Indus valley, the civilization based at *Mohenjo Daro* was established.

America had its own early civilizations: the *Maya* and *Aztec* in Mexico, *Inca* in Peru, but they did not affect people in other continents because there were no regular contacts until after Columbus discovered 'the New World' in AD 1492.

The first Europeans we hear much about were the *Greeks*—a most lively-minded, original people. They will crop up on many pages, for their ideas started so much and still affect our lives in so many ways. They did not live only in Greece and its islands. Many lived in what is now Turkey or Egypt, and in the still-famous cities they built all round the Mediterranean and the Black Sea—cities like Marseilles, Naples and Alexandria.

The *Romans* spread out their vast empire from Italy, conquering much of Europe, all North Africa, and the Middle East in Asia. When the barbarians destroyed that empire the next great conquerors were the *Arabs*, sweeping from Baghdad through North Africa into Spain. To them we owe much of our early scientific knowledge in subjects like chemistry, astronomy and mathematics.

After that period the countries begin to take on the modern names we know, so that if we say that printing started in Germany or radio began with the Italian inventor Marconi, the 'who' and 'where' are quite plain.

And of course, in one book, one cannot stop to explain everything. Any one reading this will have the wit to use an atlas or a dictionary or an encyclopaedia, to learn more if they are interested. I hope they will be.

Passing the Word

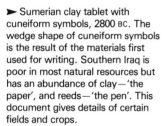

► Sumerian clay tablet with cuneiform symbols, 2800 BC. The wedge shape of cuneiform symbols is the result of the materials first used for writing. Southern Iraq is poor in most natural resources but has an abundance of clay—'the paper', and reeds—'the pen'. This document gives details of certain fields and crops.

▲ Tools of an Egyptian scribe, 2650 BC. At this stage most writing systems were cumbersome. Certainly Egyptian hieroglyphs were far too complicated for the average Egyptian to understand and the ability to read and write must have been confined to a few specially-trained scribes. The palette holds pens and inks.

▲ Using a brush to paint one of 80,000 Chinese characters. The brush was probably the earliest writing or drawing implement. Stone Age man used animal hairs bound together around a stick to paint pictures on cave walls using animal blood.

Printing

► *Diamond Sutra*, the first printed book, AD 868. Each wood block was carved out leaving a relief. This was inked and the scroll pressed onto it. The process is known as letterpress printing and remained the most popular method of printing until the mid-20th c. However carving each letter and illustration out of a woodblock was laborious. Looking for a method of

assembling them in a frame that could quickly be changed, Johann Gutenberg in the 1440s came up with a system of movable metal letter blocks with pins made from

a standard mould that could be held level in a frame. He adapted a wine press to press the frame on to the paper with even pressure (below).

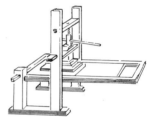

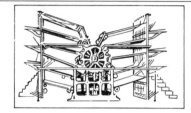

▲ Richard Hoe's Rotary Press of 1845 was used to print news-papers. The type was locked on to a central cylinder. Surrounding it were four rotating cylinders of running paper instead of one, increasing the output four times.

Writing it Down

'Make a note of that,' we say. 'It's written here in black and white.' Or, 'May I have something in writing—for the record?' It was one of the great milestones in human progress when someone hit on the idea of making marks to represent ideas. Sketch maps were probably the earliest use of markings to complement speech about 45,000 years ago. The need to count pots of grain and numbers of sheep generated a primitive accounting system in Iran about 10,700 years ago. The system used different-shaped stones to represent different commodities. It was only a matter of time (about 5000 years in Mesopotamia) before these shapes were represented by drawing them on damp clay.

Writing itself—that is markings standing for sounds that together make up words—grew out of the need to identify the name, trade and location of the owner of a particular commodity.

It was not then a question of 'black and white' because there was no paper or ink. The earliest writing we have is on clay tablets, made by the Sumerians about 3500 BC in the country that is now Iraq. While the clay was wet they scratched it with signs. These began as pictures but were gradually made simpler. They became little patterns of wedge-shaped marks. This writing is called 'cuneiform'. *Cuneus* is Latin for 'wedge'. The tablets were then baked hard.

A little later, on the other side of the world the Chinese were devising yet another system. Instead of a few different letters (like our own twenty-six today) they had thousands of separate characters, which all had to be learnt by heart. How could anyone remember an alphabetical order? And without alphabetical order how could one arrange dictionaries and telephone directories and filing systems? To hold her own in information-processing China has had to make urgent changes in the last ten years. One of these has been to develop a new alphabetical system called *pinyin* which consists of 30 phonetic characters that can easily be used in typewriters and computers.

Our own western alphabet comes to us from cuneiform though it does not look much like it. It evolved via several Middle Eastern civilizations to the Greeks and finally to the Romans. The Romans altered some of the Greek letters and then spread the alphabet all over Western Europe. The only additions were the letters J, U and W in the Middle Ages.

People had long ago begun to write on parchment made from animal skins and papyrus made from reeds. Paper—an improved process of manufacturing from fibre and cheaper than parchment—was invented by a Chinese, Tsai-Lun in AD 105, but it was hundreds of years before it spread to the West. Then, in 751, some Chinese papermakers were captured in a skirmish with the Arabs in Central Asia. They passed on the secret. Papermaking started in Samarkand and spread to the great city of Baghdad, and then across the Arab lands of North Africa into Spain and other parts of Europe.

△ A quill, the principal writing implement from 800 to 1850.

▽ Konrad Gesner's first pencil, 1565. The lead was pure graphite.

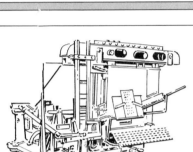

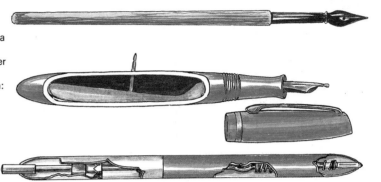

► Top: Steel pen with wooden holder. Became popular in the mid-19th c. when a hole drilled in the steel nib above the split gave a smooth flow of ink. Middle: Fountain pen. The ink-filled rubber reservoir allowed the owner to write without an ink well. Bottom: Ball-point pen with quick drying indelible ink invented by an Hungarian journalist, Josef Biro.

◄ The Linotype composing machine invented by Ottmar Mergenthaller in 1886. Typing on a keyboard, the machine moulded the letters out of molten metal and produced a solid line or 'slug' of metal type which could then be fitted into the frame of the page.

► Hammond's typewriter of 1880. A hammer hit the back of the paper pressing it against a letter on a fixed cylinder. The main disadvantage was you could not see what you had written without raising the cylinder.

► Xerox machine 1983. Photostatic copying revolutionized the printing field. Now documents can be copied quickly and cheaply in the office.

The Chinese, too, were the first printers in AD 700. They cut the characters onto a flat stone tablet, inked it, and pressed it on paper to make copies. But because of the number of Chinese characters the next stage—carving separate wooden letters and constantly rearranging them as 'movable type' to compose a new page—was not of much use to them, even though they developed the system using ceramic blocks in 1040.

It was different when the idea appeared in Europe. It may have started with the Italian cloth manufacturers using carved wooden blocks to print the same pattern all over a piece of material. It is not certain who first had the inspiration that the same thing could be done with carved wooden letters on paper, but the man usually regarded as having perfected the technique was the German, Johann Gutenberg, of Mainz. In 1455 he printed 300 copies of the Bible.

An idea which had been of little use to the Chinese was invaluable to the Europeans with their 26-letter alphabet. Until then, every book had been hand-written, one copy at a time. These methods were very slow, so there were few books, and not many people could read. Now there was no limit. Within fifty years printing presses had been set up in 183 towns, and 16,000 different works had been published in Europe. This wonderful invention helped to spread Renaissance learning round Europe and gradually many more people learned to read and write.

The Age of Learning had arrived.

▲ Newspaper print room of *The Times* working on printing plates. The curved metal plates, made from papier mâché moulds, are fixed onto a cylinder which rotates at a very high speed. The plates are inked and pressed directly on to the paper leaving the image. This type of printing is known as letterpress printing.

Sending Messages

► Pigeon post. Earliest messages were torches, bonfires and smoke signals. But these were inadequate for longer messages. Letter services have existed for centuries. But they were slow. News of the victory at the battle of Waterloo in 1815 first reached London in hours by pigeon post.

◄ Claude Chappé's semaphore telegraph, 1792. Movable shutters passed messages via a series of relay stations. A message could travel 250 km in one hour, but was dependent on clear weather.

► The 'Pony Express' operated between Missouri and California from 1860 to 1861. Relays of riders galloped the 3000 km in about 10 days carrying the mail. Two days after the first telegraph line was completed the Pony Express ceased.

Above: Samuel Morse designed a telegraph code in 1837 to carry messages in the form of pulses along a wire. In 1776 a sailing ship took seven weeks to carry the news to London that America had declared her independence. In 1855, parliament heard of Tsar Nicholas I's death the same day. Right: 1905 Telephone. The telegraph has had a much shorter life than the letter and its total decay at the hands of the telephone (and telex) is almost complete.
Below: A crystal radio set of the 1920s. The radio was invented by Marconi in 1899.

▲ Telex machine. In 1931 America introduced a telephonic system where typewriters replaced voices.

News

► Chinese soupseller, 10 BC. The Chinese empire was vast. From one side of the empire to the other was 4500 kms. It was also repressive and in order to keep a check on its far-flung outposts, the empire used a postal service to fetch and carry messages. But this service was only used by the government. Travellers brought news to the people. The most regular came to be the soupsellers who travelled all over China.

▲ Town criers were appointed to make public announcements and were important in Europe in the 16th century before newspapers.

► Newspaper boys stood on street corners shouting 'Read all about it' to attract customers to buy their papers. This boy holds a poster advertising his paper and its grim headline — the announcement of war, 3 September 1939.

▼ Two early newspapers: *The Antwerp Gazette* (left) of 17 June 1621 reporting with a picture the continuing conflict of the Thirty Years' War. The first English newspaper was a translation of this in 1622. *The Scottish Dove* (right) was a weekly paper. This edition of the week 3 November 1643 brings news of the English Civil War.

► TV newscaster, 1984. When it comes to providing a news service, TV has one main advantage over newspapers. TV can broadcast news at the time that it is happening. It is said that before the age of 18 US children watch between 10 and 15,000 hours of TV.

Spreading the News

There is money in getting the news before any one else.

Merchants knew that in the Middle Ages. Was the Emperor sick—likely to die? Would there be war? Would that mean a trade slump—or a boom in arms? But not only businessmen wanted to know what was happening. In Venice an official handwritten bulletin was posted up and people paid a small coin, a *gazzetta*, to read it, hence the word 'gazette'. Soon the Germans used their newly-developed process of printing to produce large numbers of newspapers quickly and cheaply. The first weekly newspaper—*Aviso Relation oder Zeitung*—was published in Wolfenbüttel in 1609.

Early newspapers were small and expensive, so they tended to pass from hand to hand. They could also be read in coffee-houses. Papers were serious—heavy for our modern taste—concerned mainly with the accurate reporting of politics and foreign affairs. Since they were the only source of news, the power they wielded was enormous. As the circulation of newspapers increased so did their influence and the integrity of their editors became even more important. Unhappily this integrity was often wanting. Large sums were paid to editors to support the government of the day.

One London paper still published today—*The Times* (founded in 1785)—was famous for its meticulous reporting of world affairs, but at threepence a copy was expensive. By 1850 editors had realised that there was a potentially huge market for newspapers featuring gory crime stories, scandal and gossip which at a penny a copy would be within reach of most people's pockets. Circulation of these newspapers soared to half a million copies a day and led the way to what we now call 'the popular press'. However *The Times* resisted the temptation to change its content or its price.

But *The Times* was breaking new ground in quite different ways. In 1814 it was the world's first newspaper to install steam-driven printing presses, making it possible to run off many more copies at high speed. After 1814 there were a number of crucial mechanical inventions in the printing industry (see pages 10–11). In the 1960s phototypesetting was invented which removed the need for metal type. Although most newspapers around the world use this new method, apart from *The Times* few British newspapers have been able to because of union opposition.

The Times was also the first newspaper to send its own war correspondents to give eyewitness accounts of battles. Some, like the outspoken W. H. Russell in the Crimean War (1854–6), exposed the mismanagement of the government and roused the nation to protest. Foreign correspondents became the heroes of the day. And when the telegraph was invented news could be despatched from one side of the world to the other in minutes. Journalists had become a power in the land.

This has remained the case to the present day although newspapers ceased to be the sole provider of news with the invention of radio and television.

In the 1970s labour unrest also threatened the future of newspapers in a way which would have seemed completely mad to those journalists fighting for a free uncensored press in the 18th century. However, even with these problems newspapers are still read almost as avidly as they were at their peak in the mid-1950s—293 people per thousand read them in the US and 443 per thousand in Britain.

Propaganda

PROSPECT HILL.	BUNKER's HILL.
I. Seven Dollars a Month.	I. Three Pence a Day.
II. Fresh Provisions, and in Plenty.	II. Rotten Salt Pork.
III. Health.	III. The Scurvy.
IV. Freedom, Ease, Affluence and a good Farm.	IV. Slavery, Beggary and Want.

▲ Tactical propaganda issued by American command at Prospect Hill during the battle for Boston in 1775. The leaflet is an invitation to the British troops at Bunker's Hill to desert.

► Poster of Mao Tse-tung. When Mao came to power in China in 1949 he issued many posters glamourizing himself, the might of the people and the industrial power of Communist China. The aim was to 'persuade' the Chinese that Communism was 'a good thing'.

▼ A candidate speaking from hustings at the election of 1865. It is the job of a politician to persuade a member of the electorate to vote for him. Today TV and radio are used enormously but still there is no substitute for the live speech and all politicians recognize this as part of any election campaign.

Above: Red Russian cartoon of 1919 implying that France and Britain manipulated the White Russian generals like dogs before their overthrow by the Red Russians or *bolsheviks*. The implication being that any régime that is not powerful enough to stand alone is not worth having.

Above right: Josef Goebbels. Perhaps the greatest propagandist who ever lived. He was responsible for the campaign that swept Hitler into power and kept him there.

Right: 1979 Health Education Council poster. Propaganda is not always subversive or political.

Travel and Transport

Highway and Railway

In terms of mobility on land early man differed little from animals. By and large they relied on their legs to get from A to B. Domestication of animals (see p.75) and the wheel changed that. By 5800 BC it had become clear that cattle could serve a more useful purpose than just as providers of meat, they could pull loads. At first these were ploughs and sledges, but eventually (2000–2500 years later) the imaginative leap was made and we had the wheel. However the draught animal is the crucial factor in emphasizing the usefulness of the wheel. For example the wheel was known in the ancient New World but it could not be exploited because there were no suitable draught animals. The wheel changed ancient industrial society. Suddenly fuel and raw materials, which had seemed impossibly distant became a day's cart-ride away.

The horse was domesticated at about the same time as the ox but for an inexplicably long time was not considered to be as efficient as the ox. It seems that for 2000 years nobody noticed that the ox harness used by horses pinched the horse's windpipe, dramatically reducing its effectiveness. So until 250 BC when a Chinese invented the breast strap and then the horse collar (250 years later) horses were used as pack animals and for riding.

Before long improvements were made to the roads to maximize the horse's potential. Civilizations before the Romans had produced roads of quality and length but it was the Romans who made them a priority. It was possible to ride from one end of the Roman empire to the other in weeks where before it had taken years. The roads were not built just to smash records, it was the only way so large an empire could be administered. When that empire fell it was over 1000 years before the world had such roads again.

Good roads inspired new ideas in transport. As trade possibilities increased, so did the different means of carriage. Waggons were the most successful method. Carts had always existed but now comfort and manoeuvrability were added to the basic design. The village of Kocs in Hungary, on the Danube at a crossroad between Europe and Asia, grew famous for making them. In the late 15th century its skilled craftsmen devised a new type, with two smaller front-wheels for easier turning, and a basket-work body roofed with leather. It was called, from the name of the village, a 'coach'. Orders came from foreign countries, especially when the Hungarians added two improvements for greater comfort—slings on which the body of the vehicle swung clear of the bumps in the road, and

Getting About

Above: Sled used by the Babylonians, 2000 BC. By this time the wheel was in common use, but this sled would have been more efficient over rough ground. The first sleds were used in N. Mesopotamia in 5800 BC.
Below: Two-wheeled cart, 2000 BC. Heavy loads were first rolled on logs. The first wheel was probably a section cut off a log with a hole drilled in the middle for an axle.

◀ The wheelbarrow was invented in China in the 3rd century AD and was first used to transport people.

▶ A Celtic ceremonial waggon of AD 100 used on feast days. Note the improved breast harness for the horse.

▼ Chinese sedan chair, AD 125. Carried by four servants a rich man could get from A to B in privacy and comfort.

▼ The jaunting cart of Ireland (below) has a seat above each wheel.

Public Transport

▲ Royal Mail coach, 1820. The fastest vehicle on the road, it travelled at 16 km/h while carrying 9 passengers.

▲ Rickshaws were first widely used in the Far East in the 1870s.

▲ Omnibuses (1880) carried 40 passengers and cost a shilling for 6 kms.

then springs, which cushioned the passengers still further.

All this changed within a generation after the first railway began in 1825 running between Stockton and Darlington. When the steam engine was invented, several people tried to use it to drive a road carriage—but the roads were too bad. Then a British engineer, Richard Trevithick, thought of mounting a steam carriage on rails to give a smoother ride. The idea came from the mining industry, where iron tracks were used to make the heavy coal trucks move more easily. Within 25 years of the first railway, almost every country in Europe had built one. Enough railway track had been laid to stretch around the world. Soon, people could travel across Europe. It took a little longer to build tracks across the vaster distances—to cross the prairies and the Rocky Mountains to the Pacific or to link the great cities of India—but with colossal energy and ingenuity it was done. The lives of countless millions were transformed.

But another form of transport was being invented that would one day threaten the survival of the railway, too. In 1863 a Belgian, Lenoir, demonstrated a 'motor car' with an internal combustion engine. Further work by the Germans Karl Benz and Gottlieb Daimler had, by the 1890s, really put the automobile on the road, and when Henry Ford introduced mass-production to his car factories in America, the world was soon filled with cars.

▲ Body line at the Ford factory in Dagenham, England in 1938. In 1908 Henry Ford began mass producing his Model T in America making the car cheaper so that by 1913 there were 1 million cars on US roads, 200,000 in Britain and 90,000 in France. By 1939 Henry Ford owned everything that was required to make cars from the iron ore mines to the selling agencies. The automobile industry is now the world's largest and currently employs about 35 million people worldwide.

▲ The brougham was made for Lord Brougham in 1839—one of the first closed private carriages.

▼ American buggy, 1850.

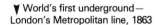

▲ Karl von Drais' dandyhorse, 1817. It had no pedals.

▼ Hildebrand and Wolfmüller motorcycle, 1894. First to be sold commercially, it was powered by a water-cooled twin cylinder engine.

▲ 1909 Model T Ford, known as the 'Tin Lizzie'. It was cheap to run, easy to maintain and had a top speed of 64 km/h. Between 1908 and 1927 over 15 million were sold.

▼ The Modulo was built in 1969 by Pininfarina (Italy). The roof and windscreen slide forward for access. There is an adjustable front aerofoil and the car has broad tyres.

▼ World's first underground— London's Metropolitan line, 1863

▲ Electric tram (1890) provided the first cheap and reliable urban transport.

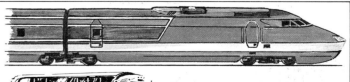

▲ The North American Greyhound bus company provides cheap fast travel across all the US.

▲ French prototype high-speed turbo train, TGV, designed for speeds up to 306 km/h. Its engines are aircraft type gas turbines. The world's fastest train is the French aerotrain at 375 km/h.

Travel by Water

Navigation

▶ Dugout canoe, 8000 BC. The earliest boats were made from materials that grew nearby. So in the north where forests prevail boats tend to be made using logs, while in the Middle East where trees are scarce reeds plaited together are used.

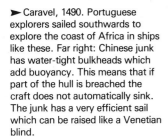

▲ Coracle, 6000 BC. Originally from Wales made using animal skins fixed to a wooden frame. Still used in the Welsh hills, tarred canvas has replaced the animal skin.

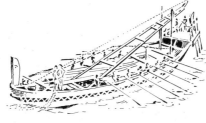

▲ Egyptian ship, 3000 BC. Built from wood blocks pegged together. A taut rope ran from stem to stern over crutches to stop the hull breaking in half.

▶ Caravel, 1490. Portuguese explorers sailed southwards to explore the coast of Africa in ships like these. Far right: Chinese junk has water-tight bulkheads which add buoyancy. This means that if part of the hull is breached the craft does not automatically sink. The junk has a very efficient sail which can be raised like a Venetian blind.

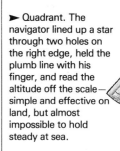

▶ Mississippi sternwheeler, 1820. These boats were home for the most notorious gamblers, betting on cards and the outcome of the famous Mississippi river races which were extremely dangerous. Striving for speed, boilers frequently exploded and from 1810 to 1850 an estimated 4000 people died in steamboat disasters.

Above: Steamship *Great Eastern* designed by Isambard Kingdom Brunel and launched in 1858. Designed to carry 4000 passengers she was under-powered, although she had sails, paddles and propellers. She spent her short working life as a cable layer. Below right: The clipper *Cutty Sark*, 1869, so-called because such ships 'clipped' time off the schedules. They reached speeds of 20 knots.

▼ The high speed of hydrofoil craft makes them ideal for passenger service over short routes and calm waters. The first hydrofoil was built in 1906 and in 1918 Alexander Graham Bell built a hydrofoil that reached 114 km/h.

▶ Traverse board used to record compass directions and speed taken at intervals during a 4 hour watch on deck. From it, the ship's course could be plotted on a chart.

▶ Quadrant. The navigator lined up a star through two holes on the right edge, held the plumb line with his finger, and read the altitude off the scale— simple and effective on land, but almost impossible to hold steady at sea.

▼ A cross staff measured the angle between the horizon and the sun determining how far north you were.

▶ Arab astrolabe (1700s) had the same function as the cross staff with the arm at the centre lining up with the sun. But a lurching ship made it difficult to use.

▼ Sextant. The navigator sights the horizon through the eye-piece (below left), moves the index arm (with the index mirror) until he also sees the sun (middle), adjusts the image of the sun, by moving the index arm, until it 'sits' on the horizon (right), reads the sun's altitude off the calibrated arm.

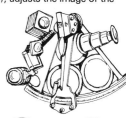

▶ Navigation buoys were used as early as 1000. This example dates from the 1880s. Many modern buoys look like this, but have radar beacons and electronic aids for even greater safety.

All Aboard

In Australia, there are traces of early man from 40 thousand years ago. Even allowing for the low sea level during the ice age there must have been a stretch of open ocean about 90 km wide separating Australia from Indonesia which had to be crossed. So man had some sort of seafaring craft from the earliest times.

The very first 'boats' must have been logs straddled by man paddling with his hands or a piece of wood, to cross a river maybe 2 million years ago. In time people learned to hollow out the log with tools or fire, and to shape proper paddles. It was worth the trouble for then they could use the boat for travelling up and down the river as well as crossing it.

Paddling came first. Rowing, with long oars to give more power, came later as boats grew bigger and broader, and were made of reeds or of planks fitted closely together and made watertight. At first the rowers faced the way they were going. Then it was found that they could exert more power if they rowed backwards—provided there was a man steering.

For many centuries the steering was done with an oar or paddle at the stern. The Vikings, those great Scandinavian voyagers who roved the seas from about AD 780 onwards, had this oar on the right, and to this day this side of the ship is called 'starboard', from 'stern board'. In port, the Vikings moored with the left side against the wharf—hence the 'port' side. A hinged sternpost rudder was not used in Europe until about AD 1200, or rather, at first, two rudders. When the Italian traveller Marco Polo reached China in 1298 he was very impressed with the ships there, and surprised to find that the Chinese were using a single rudder and had been doing so for 400 years or more!

Although both the Vikings and the Mediterranean nations had kept oars for propelling their long galleys, sails had been in use from at least 5000 BC. At first it was only a single square sail, and could be used only if the wind was blowing astern. But gradually improvements were made, both in sails and in ship-design generally, and the ancient navigators—Egyptians, Phoenicians, Greeks and others—made very long voyages, sometimes into unknown seas, while the Vikings in 1000 reached as far as America.

The opening up of the east by Marco Polo and others led to the introduction in the 15th century of two Chinese inventions into the navies of Europe—three masts, which increased the speed of a vessel, and the magnetic compass, which allowed a course to be followed more accurately than ever before. With these improvements first the Spanish and Portuguese, then the Dutch, English and French opened up the oceans of the world. For the next four centuries sailing ships became bigger, better and faster, culminating in graceful clippers like the *Cutty Sark* (1869). They were mainly used for cargo—for passenger-travel their days had passed.

Steam had taken over. The idea of a steamship first occurred to a French doctor, Denis Papin, in 1685. But it was not until 1783 that another Frenchman, the Marquis de Jouffroy d'Abbans, built a steam-driven paddle-wheeler and took it upstream from Lyons on the River Saône. The Americans started the first steamboat service, on the Delaware river in 1790. Subsequently they built the first boat with screw-propellers (1804) and achieved both the first sea-voyage by steam (1809) and the first Atlantic crossing (1819). All these early sea-going vessels had masts and sails, to be on the safe side.

Quickly now the steamship took over the passenger trade. It was swift and reliable—and the boilers did not explode causing terrible fires as nervous people had feared. Such people were further reassured by another far-reaching change. They had feared that a ship would sink if it was made of iron. In 1822 the first iron-built steamship crossed from England to France —with a cargo of iron. Ships no longer had to be made of inflammable timber.

Until the 19th century people travelling by sea had been dependent on cargo-vessels willing to take passengers. Now came the liners, catering primarily for them. The first regular trans-Atlantic liner was Brunel's *Great Western*, which in 1838 sailed from Bristol to New York in just over 15 days, with accommodation for 240 passengers. For the next hundred years liners grew more luxurious, until they became like floating hotels.

Today the swiftest steamship is a snail compared with an aeroplane. So the proud liners that remain have become cruise-ships, used—as sailing craft are—for pleasure rather than for just getting to places. But this applies mainly to the long journeys. It would be wrong to imagine that the passenger-vessel has lost all its usefulness. All over the world—in the Greek islands, along sparsely populated coasts like those of Norway or Western Scotland, and on countless rivers, lakes and inland seas—the local steamer serves the population like a local bus. Though strickly speaking, it is probably not a 'steamer' any more—but oil-powered.

▼ The Australian 12m Yacht *Australia*. The predecessor of *Australia II* which so famously wrested the America's Cup from the United States in 1983.

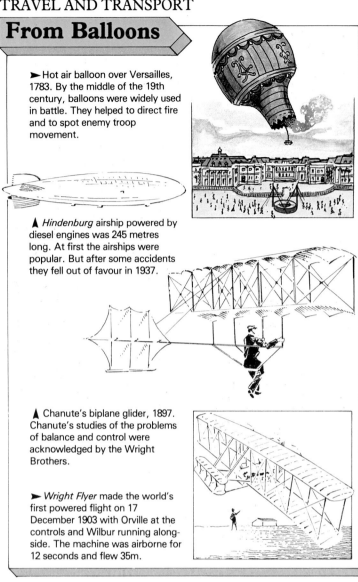

From Balloons

► Hot air balloon over Versailles, 1783. By the middle of the 19th century, balloons were widely used in battle. They helped to direct fire and to spot enemy troop movement.

▲ *Hindenburg* airship powered by diesel engines was 245 metres long. At first the airships were popular. But after some accidents they fell out of favour in 1937.

▲ Chanute's biplane glider, 1897. Chanute's studies of the problems of balance and control were acknowledged by the Wright Brothers.

► *Wright Flyer* made the world's first powered flight on 17 December 1903 with Orville at the controls and Wilbur running alongside. The machine was airborne for 12 seconds and flew 35m.

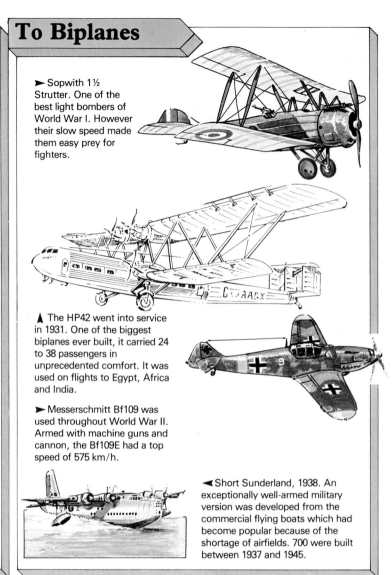

To Biplanes

► Sopwith 1½ Strutter. One of the best light bombers of World War I. However their slow speed made them easy prey for fighters.

▲ The HP42 went into service in 1931. One of the biggest biplanes ever built, it carried 24 to 38 passengers in unprecedented comfort. It was used on flights to Egypt, Africa and India.

► Messerschmitt Bf109 was used throughout World War II. Armed with machine guns and cannon, the Bf109E had a top speed of 575 km/h.

◄ Short Sunderland, 1938. An exceptionally well-armed military version was developed from the commercial flying boats which had become popular because of the shortage of airfields. 700 were built between 1937 and 1945.

The Conquest of the Air

When the writer of this book was born it was barely three weeks since the first aeroplane had flown across the English Channel. Just before his sixtieth birthday, in 1969, the first men landed on the Moon. In less than a lifetime our ancient dream of flying had been fulfilled and developed with a speed beyond all reasonable expectation.

The human race dreamed of flight as soon as they began to watch birds. That Italian genius, Leonardo da Vinci, had believed that human muscle-power could achieve it with artificial bird-like wings. But the right design could not be discovered. Every experiment ended in farce or tragedy. Leonardo was mistaken. To lift a man off the ground and keep him air-borne some stronger power was essential. An air-filled balloon was the first source to be harnessed by the Montgolfier brothers in 1783 using a paper balloon. But a balloon could only drift where the air currents took it and was therefore very dangerous.

It was obvious that any power source must of itself be light in weight, so that when a new power source was invented—the steam engine—it was of no use to the would-be aviator. The breakthrough came with the internal combustion engine that drove the motor car. Within a few years far-sighted

▲ Howard Hughes' American wooden flying boat 'Spruce Goose'. It was originally conceived as a means of flying vast quantities of men and equipment across the Atlantic to the allies, avoiding German U-boats. Completed in 1947, it was (and remains) the largest aircraft ever built with a wingspan of 97.5 metres. To prove to his critics that it could fly, the eccentric Hughes flew it, but only once—a flight of one mile (1.6 km) at an altitude of 21m and then put it into storage where it has remained.

From Jets

▲ Avro Lancaster. British 4-engine bomber. In all 7366 made 156,000 missions dropping 618,350 tonnes of bombs in World War II.

► The Douglas DC-3, 1936— the world's most successful airliner. Well over 10,000 were built and many are still flying.

▼ Harrier GR1 (below) became the world's first vertical take-off warplane, 1969.
Concorde (bottom)—a masterpiece of supersonic design, it can travel at twice the speed of sound. The first man to break the sound barrier was Chuck Yeager (US) in 1947.

To Space

Above: Bristol 171 Helicopter. The first efficient helicopters appeared in 1950. Their ability to hover makes them perfect for rescue work.
Right Middle: The Orbiter Columbia (USA) returns to earth after its first flight in 1981. In years to come these rocket planes will make many return trips into space leading to space station construction and space tourism.
Right Below: Tornado swingwing is an advanced, heavily-armed, combat aircraft. Its most striking features are its foolproof weapon aiming system and its electronic counter-measure equipment which makes it virtually immune to all but the most sophisticated weapons.

Below: Blackbird (US), one of the world's most successful reconnaissance aircraft. It can cruise for 2 hours, 24 km up at 3220 km/h.

inventors saw that a similar engine might be strong enough to lift a flying machine off the ground, without itself adding excessive weight. Two American brothers built such a machine, fitting it with a 12-horsepower, 4-cylinder petrol engine and two propellers. On December 17, 1903, they tried it out. Orville Wright stayed in the air for only a few seconds, then Wilbur for almost a minute. It worked! Man had taken his first steps in his conquest of the air.

A year or two later their improved model flew 38 km. And then, incredibly, the brothers lost interest. It was the French who went on experimenting, and Louis Blériot's flight from France to England on July 25, 1909 captured everybody's imagination.

Had it not been for World War I, the development of air travel might have been very slow because of the massive expense necessary for research, but for war, governments will always find money. When the fighting started the aeroplane was found to be even more important than they had realized, so millions of pounds were poured out to improve machines. Early 'dog-fights' between airmen included shooting at each other with pistols, like cowboys. By 1918, after over four years of combat, both sides had thousands of aircraft, with technical improvements that in peacetime would have taken more than forty years. The Germans had also had some success with airships, bombing Britain with their zeppelins. After the war, the idea of comfortable civilian airships was popular, but after two terrible disasters no more were built.

The knowledge, gained so quickly during the war, went straight into the development of air travel. The world's first regular daily service was started between Berlin and Weimar in February, 1919. Within weeks came the first international service, Paris to Brussels, and by the summer one between London and Paris. By the end of that first year of peace, services were springing up everywhere. More comfortable seating in cabins, and cooked meals quickly followed. The first air hostess (an American nurse who herself suggested the idea) appeared in 1930.

The second World War, like the first, quickened technical changes. The idea of a jet engine, with a massive backward thrust from air and ignited fuel, instead of propellers, occurred to the Englishman, Frank Whittle, and the German, Ernst Heinkel, at about the same time in 1930, and in the opening week of the war, in 1939, Hitler had the first jet aircraft ready, the Heinkel 178. Ten years later Britain flew the first jet airliner. A quite different form of technical advance—in computers—was meanwhile preparing the way for satellites and space-ships, in which Russians and Americans became tireless rivals.

The benefits of air travel are incalculable. Families split by continents can now visit each other whereas in bygone days they might have expected only to have communicated by letter. Today in 48 hours people can travel round the world; in 1800 you would have been lucky to complete the journey between London and York.

Travelling in Style

▲ Egyptian gondola, 1375 BC. All rulers and rich Egyptians lived close to the Nile, so most travel was by boat. Short boat journeys would have been made more bearable by provisions of fruit and wine.

► Decorated Indian elephant. The elephant driver guides the animal by giving it signals behind its ears with his feet. Protected from the sun, the passengers' journey is extremely comfortable.

► Italian sedan chair, about 1730. Privately owned chairs were richly ornamented and painted by famous artists. Often they had a large coat of arms so that the identity of the passenger was never left in doubt.

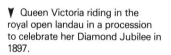

▲ Montezuma, king of the Aztecs being carried on a litter, 1518. All members of the royal family were carried. No-one is allowed to look at Montezuma nor speak to him, on pain of death.

▼ Queen Victoria riding in the royal open landau in a procession to celebrate her Diamond Jubilee in 1897.

▲ A British officer in India carried through the streets in a palanquin. Many officials were notorious for their greed and arrogance. In England these 'nabobs' were hated for their vulgar display.

▼ Luxurious interior of the Rolls Royce Phantom VI motor car. It contains a TV, radio, drinks cabinet, telephone and bullet-proof glass.

▼ A first-class dining car on the Great Northern railway, 1879.

Hotels and Inns

► Roman tavern selling red wine, cheese and bread, AD 25. The tavern keeper usually had some rooms above the shop for rent.

▼ Monasteries were the first 'hotels', 1300. Travellers were always welcome to stay in the hospital, which meant place of hospitality (the sick were looked after in the Infirmary).

▲ Caravanserai in Iran provided shelter for the camel caravans that travelled to and fro across the desert, busily trading.

◄ Hotel de la Tour at Martigny, Switzerland was much patronized on Thomas Cook's tours, 1870s. His tours led to a rapid increase in hotel building in Switzerland.

▲ Grand Hotel, Naples. This beautiful 19th-century Italian hotel shows the luxury awaiting the traveller of that time. It still stands today, a haven from the heat and dust of that bustling city.

► Bonaventura Hotel, Los Angeles. Today the outside of a hotel is as important as the interior. A brilliant design affords considerable status.

Seeing the World

Travelling for pleasure seems to have begun with the ancient Greeks—like many other good ideas. Herodotus, who died in 425 BC, is called 'the Father of History', but his famous account of the Persian Wars was just as much a travel-book. He spent years wandering about the Mediterranean countries and the Middle East, eager to see everything and observe the strange ways of foreign peoples.

In the Roman Empire it was very easy to travel. There were splendid roads and inns, innumerable ships sailing to and fro, the same government over the whole area, and most people able to understand either Latin or Greek, if not both.

There was already a tourist industry, with guides eager to show off the local sights. Pausanias, a Greek who lived at this period, travelled widely and wrote a guide-book describing great buildings and other features that have long since vanished. Besides sightseeing there were popular holiday centres. At the springs of Clitumnus (an Italian beauty-spot near Assisi) the Roman Pliny tells us of a local organization 'to maintain the bathing station and provide lodgings for visitors.'

In the Middle Ages, people made long pilgrimages to holy shrines. Many did so because they were religious and longed to see Jerusalem or Rome or some other sacred place. But many (as Chaucer hints in his poem about the pilgrims riding to Canterbury) found it a good excuse to see the world and enjoy themselves.

It was all highly organized, especially the trip to Jerusalem. Parties from northern Europe would make for Venice where, in the season, you could book your return fare to the Holy Land. You could even hire bedding for the trip, with a refund if you survived to bring it back. At the other end, the ship's captain would arrange guides and donkeys for the journey inland. And, of course, you could buy souvenirs (often fakes) and badges to show you had been there.

After the Middle Ages a new fashion in travel began. Young gentlemen, after school and university, were sent off to tour Europe and complete their education. The phrase, 'the Grand Tour', first appeared in 1679, but such travel had been common for nearly a hundred years by then. The main destination was Italy, then the country where there was most to learn. A *vetturino* or carriage-driver would provide a sort of package-tour. For an agreed sum he would take you from, say, Florence to Rome, paying for your lodging and meals.

Even for the rich, travel was slow, uncomfortable and even dangerous until the coming of railways, steamers and hotels. After that, there was no need for a 'once-in-a-lifetime' grand tour—people could travel whenever they pleased. And the imagination of Thomas Cook, first of the travel agents, brought in a much wider public. In 1861 he organized his first mass package-holiday for 1700 working-class customers, taking them from London to Paris and back, with five nights' accommodation (choice of 13 hotels) and all meals, for 46 shillings (£2.30p) each—very cheap indeed.

English passports are first recorded in 1414. They were handwritten permits obtained from the Privy Council. They allowed you to 'pass the port' out of the country but then you needed another passport from the King of France or whatever country you entered. Today your only passport is that of your own government and if you need special permission to enter a foreign territory you apply for a 'visa' stamp in your passport.

War and Armaments

The Causes of War

It has been said that it is our instinct to fight and many human beings do quarrel and have fights. However, they seldom kill anyone. Still less do they long to kill people they do not know or to form armies for that purpose.

Nevertheless, for some reason, they have often done so. We need to understand those reasons if only so that we can work to remove them.

Greed is one, sheer need is another. Even prehistoric men must have conflicted over the best hunting-grounds and fishing areas. They may sometimes have fought over women.

When people learned to keep flocks and herds, to grow crops and build towns, there was much more to fight over—much more that the strong could be tempted to take from the weak. Soon it was not just a question of the wild, undisciplined people attacking the civilized—the civilized were building up bigger and bigger empires with a new form of greed, not only for plunder but for wider territory, captured slaves, and the desire for power and glory. Alexander the Great marched his Greek army as far as India in his dream to conquer the world. He died on the return journey, his dream unfulfilled, and his empire disintegrated.

The Romans with their disciplined legions fought countless wars and built a much more durable empire. When that collapsed after lasting for centuries, fresh wars of conquest by the barbarian Goths, the Arabs and the Turks, created fresh empires, and a quite different kind of conquering power was wielded by the less disciplined Mongol hordes, bloodthirsty, well-armed horsemen who swept out of Central Asia. For much of the Middle Ages these nomads threatened eastern Europe, the Near East and even far-off China.

The age of explorations from the 15th century onwards revealed riches around the world beyond the imagination of most Europeans. Within two hundred years European colonies had sprung up in the east and west, each country hoping to become rich on the commodities to be found there.

As trade became more important, nations started to fight for 'markets'—to knock out their business rivals in some region and get all the profits of trading there. In Asia the British fought such wars against the Portuguese, the Dutch and the French. Countries sought to control oilfields (as in the Persian Gulf) or rice-supplies or rubber. To make sure of them, they

often ended by conquering the whole country. Even barren scraps of ground might be a cause for war if they were 'key positions', suitable for naval and air bases to protect other possessions. The Cuban crisis of 1961 and Pearl Harbor in 1942 are both examples of conflict for strategic purposes.

In modern times, the two main causes or excuses for war are religion and politics. These causes are not new. When in the 7th century, the Arabs swept triumphantly across North Africa and into Spain, and eastwards as far as central Asia, it was the new faith of Islam that inspired them. In our own day Jew has fought with Muslim, and Muslim with Hindu. On the political front, revolutions have wrenched power from the rich so that the poor could have a better life. Today the war in Afghanistan is another in a series of communist/capitalist conflicts that have blighted the world for the last forty years and will continue to do so for many years to come.

The nuclear bomb has introduced an entirely new element into modern warfare—nuclear deterrent—the idea that there is no point in Russia or America launching a nuclear attack on each other as the attacker would be destroyed too. However, with estimates showing that by the end of the 1980s at least 16 countries will have nuclear weapons, the possibility of nuclear war does not diminish.

Gone are the days when a day would be fixed for the battle, and the fighting postponed if the enemy were not ready. Today it is often not possible to distinguish between the winner and the loser and it is not surprising that more and more people are beginning to query the motives and consequences of war.

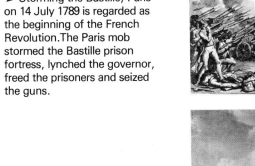

◄ Pearl Harbor 7 December 1941. The USS *Virginia* and *Tennessee* after the Japanese attack. The purpose of the attack was to knock out the strategically valuable US naval base in the Pacific Ocean.

► Storming the Bastille, Paris on 14 July 1789 is regarded as the beginning of the French Revolution.The Paris mob stormed the Bastille prison fortress, lynched the governor, freed the prisoners and seized the guns.

▲ This picture of a fully-armed Israeli soldier praying at the Wailing Wall in Jerusalem gently shows the hypocrisy of war.

▼ The Roman general Trajan had a column erected in the first century AD to glorify his achievements in the Dacian campaigns of central Europe. The column is 42 metres high.

► Battle of Ter Heyde, August 1653. General Monk finally defeated the Dutch Admiral Tromp (who was shot during the attack), after a series of English defeats at the hands of the Dutch in various trade wars. Peace was concluded the following year.

The Warrior and his Weapons

Warriors have always wanted better weapons. Weapons which allow them to kill faster and from further away. Ancient fighting meant hitting the enemy at close quarters with a club, axe, spear or sword. Missiles have also been used from the earliest days of warfare—stones, throwing-spears, arrows, bullets, cannon balls, explosive shells and, most recently, the inter-continental rocket.

Weapons changed to suit the particular needs of an army. For instance the Egyptians developed a Sumerian invention—the chariot, and used it, from about 1550 BC, to overrun all the neighbouring countries. For a thousand years it was the chariot-charge that won battles.

In Greece, however, the mountains made chariots useless. The Greeks worked out a compact infantry formation, the phalanx—dense ranks of men with six-metre spears. With the disciplined charge of the phalanx Alexander the Great shattered even the teeming hosts of Persia.

The Romans improved on this with a more flexible formation, the legion. Instead of long spears each man had two shorter javelins to throw. They were made so that the

▲ The nuclear-powered aircraft carrier *Nimitz* was built by the US Navy in 1971. Fully loaded, with her complement of 6300 men, including the aviation staff to man the 90 aircraft and helicopters, she weighs 92,950 tonnes. After World War II, it was thought that the day for these immense carriers was over, but it has proved otherwise. A task force based on such a vessel can be sent swiftly to any trouble centre in the world. The nuclear reactors which power the *Nimitz* have energy for 13 years of naval operations.

Hand Weapons

▼ Iron Celtic sword, 300 BC. When men learned to smelt and forge iron it soon took the place of bronze for making weapons.

▼ The spiked mace was so massive that it would crack armour, 1200. This one is called a 'morning star' mace. Some warlike churchmen, who were forbidden to draw blood by using a sword felt quite free to brain an enemy with a mace.

▲ Stone Age spear. Used by Eskimo and Australian aborigines until modern times.

Artillery

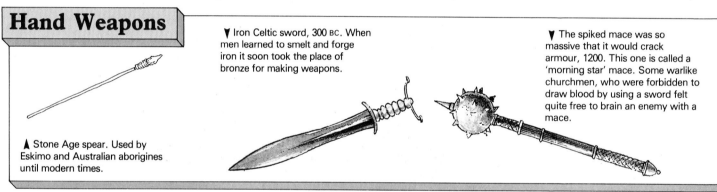

A Welsh longbow.

▲ The sling was a leather strap shaped to hold a stone, which flew out at great velocity when the sling was twirled.

▲ The crossbow was loaded by winding the string back with handles. The archer put one foot in a kind of stirrup to brace himself.

Projectiles

▼ Early type of cannon as used at Crécy in 1354. A stone cannon-ball was put in with tow and gun-powder and ignited by taper.

► US Field-gun, 1861–1865. Gun-fire was accurate, so trenches and fortifications grew more important, cavalry charges less so.

►Giant catapults and similar siege-engines were used from about 400 BC. Skeins of twisted hair and gut provided the power—they were wound up and then suddenly let go, hurling missiles with immense velocity. Some used rocks, others shot javelins.

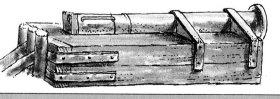

point bent or snapped on impact. So if you hit your enemy he had an even uglier wound. If you missed him, the javelin was no use to throw back at you. Over the next 600 years the legions turned most of Europe and the Middle East into the Roman Empire—and held it.

The supremacy of the foot soldier came to an end through a simple device—the stirrup. Up to that date the cavalry rode without stirrups. A man could not strike with full force—he fell off too easily. The barbarian horsemen of Asia used stirrups from before 300 BC but it was not until AD 378, at Adrianople in Turkey, that the Emperor Valens and his legions met Gothic cavalry equipped in this way. Valens, all his senior officers, and 40,000 soldiers were wiped out. For the next thousand years the armoured horseman, rock-firm and braced in his stirrups, dominated the battlefield.

A foot soldier's best chance was to shoot the horseman from a distance. But the early bows were rather feeble. And the deadly crossbow, in use in about AD 850, took so long to wind up and reload that it was really only successful in sieges. With the introduction of the Welsh longbow, nearly two metres long, a good archer could loose ten arrows a minute—and they would pierce armour, muscle, bone, saddle and into the horse beneath. The English kings enlisted the Welsh archers, who mowed down the Scottish knights at Falkirk in 1298 and the French at Crecy in 1346, and after. The longbow required strong muscles and constant practice.

Throughout this period, engineers were attempting to perfect gunpowder as a means of propelling missiles, and by 1500 cannons and handguns were improving. In 1595 the English government officially gave up the longbow, though it was still much faster and more accurate than the musket, which took two minutes to fire once and reload.

Since then, fire-arms have steadily developed in range, power and accuracy. Weapons like the Kentucky rifle (1725) enabled the American colonists to win their independence against the British redcoats and their muskets. Later came the machine-gun and the automatic rifle. Meantime the 'big guns' have evolved by land and sea, until there are giant rockets that can reach to another continent.

► By AD 1500 gunpowder which previously had been loose and therefore dangerous was stored in waxed paper cylinders. Today's bullets or cartridges (right) have a copper-coated lead bullet which is fixed in a brass case containing the powder. When the percussion cap in the base of the bullet is hit by the hammer it detonates causing the powder to explode.

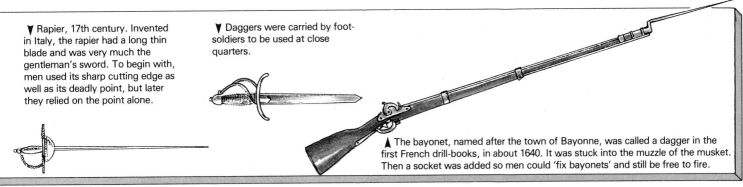

▼ Rapier, 17th century. Invented in Italy, the rapier had a long thin blade and was very much the gentleman's sword. To begin with, men used its sharp cutting edge as well as its deadly point, but later they relied on the point alone.

▼ Daggers were carried by foot-soldiers to be used at close quarters.

▲ The bayonet, named after the town of Bayonne, was called a dagger in the first French drill-books, in about 1640. It was stuck into the muzzle of the musket. Then a socket was added so men could 'fix bayonets' and still be free to fire.

▲ 16th-century matchlock musket. The match was a slow-burning cord which touched the priming powder, which set off the main charge of powder in the barrel, expelling the bullet.

▼ Colt revolver, 1835, invented by Samuel Colt in America before he was 21. It held six cartridges in a revolving magazine. First used by US troops against Indians, it became the cowboy's favourite weapon.

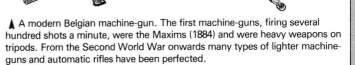

▲ A modern Belgian machine-gun. The first machine-guns, firing several hundred shots a minute, were the Maxims (1884) and were heavy weapons on tripods. From the Second World War onwards many types of lighter machine-guns and automatic rifles have been perfected.

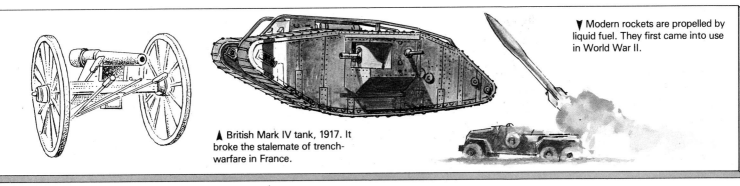

▲ British Mark IV tank, 1917. It broke the stalemate of trench-warfare in France.

▼ Modern rockets are propelled by liquid fuel. They first came into use in World War II.

WILLIAMSTON HIGH SCHOOL

The Art of Self-Defence

Men have always sought shelter from attack behind defences of wood and earth, brick and stone. The splendid city of Byzantium had a 20-kilometre wall. The Great Wall of China stretched 2500 kilometres. Castles and forts innumerable have been built throughout history.

The builders of castles made walls thicker and towers higher, so that they could always shoot down at the enemy. They built towers projecting from the ramparts, so that archers could aim sideways at those besiegers who were invisible from immediately above. Arrow-slits were designed so narrow that even the finest marksman below could never pierce them.

Medieval castles became more complicated. Moats, spanned by drawbridges, kept the attackers at a distance. Gates, already massive, could be instantly covered by dropping the portcullis, a grille of timber and iron. If the attackers reached the archway and fancied they were safe from being shot at, men in the gatehouse overhead could rain down stones and boiling oil through openings called 'murder holes'. Many castles were never taken until cannon became good enough to blast holes in them. After that, low and squat fortresses were designed, embedded in the ground. Today the favourite protection is the subterranean bunker.

As men often had to fight in the open they sought protection using armour. Helmets and shields were the most common, found literally 'from China to Peru'. Modern policemen still use helmets and even riot-shields. Shields varied greatly. Assyrian archers had tall wicker shields. The Egyptians stretched bull hide over a wooden frame and added copper studs. The Romans began with oval shields, but changed to a curved oblong shape which could be interlocked to make an unbroken battle-line—the testudo. The Anglo Saxons had round ones. The Normans favoured a long kite shape which covered the leg when on horseback.

The first armour was made of padded cloth or leather. The Japanese samurai wore very light, flexible armour, with hundreds of lacquered iron scales linked by silken cords. Mail was widely worn: iron rings were either stitched to a long shirt or interlinked as in a chain. A mail hauberk took much time and skill to make. It might cost as much as two horses.

But mail could be pierced by longbows. So knights changed to plate armour, skilfully shaped to the body and jointed so that the wearer could move freely. A fine suit of armour was a work of art, but it was exhausting to walk in.

A soldier's best protection is often neither armour nor fortification, but knowing what the enemy plans to do. Scouts and spies have been vital from the earliest times down to the satellite cameras and other scientific devices of today.

Tactics

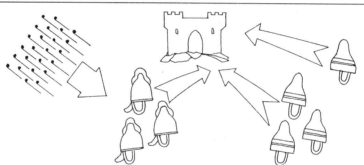

► In the Greek phalanx the heavy-armed infantry formed up in close lines, one behind another, so that their long spears projected in front of the first rank and made a hedge of bristling points. The phalanx did not have to stand still—it could march forward and even charge, carrying all before it.

◄ Siege. When besieging a town or castle, the general must look out for enemy armies marching to relieve it. So, while some of his troops were blockading or battering the defences, he had to keep a reserve force ready to drive off an outside attack.

Defence

◄ Maiden Castle—one of the biggest hill-top forts of Iron Age Europe, built about 300 BC in southern England. The encircling terraces of ramparts, once 25 metres high, can still be seen.

► Rochester Castle looms 30 metres above the River Medway in Kent, and is a fine example of the square Norman keep built all over England.

Armour

◄ A Roman legionary had an iron helmet and over his woollen tunic armour of overlapping iron scales. Below the belt he relied mainly on the protection of his shield.

► Roman testudo—the Latin word for tortoise—was a way of advancing under a hail of arrows and stones. It meant moving as one man to keep the overlapping shields in position.

► Leather armour offered tough protection from the time of the Sumerian foot-soldiers in c. 2900 BC, here, to that of the archers at Agincourt in 1415.

►Fylingdales, in Yorkshire, is one of the three BMEWS (Ballistic Missile Early Warning System) radar stations established in the late 1950s. They increase the range for tracking ballistic missiles to about 5000 km. The other stations are in Greenland and Alaska. The distant enemy missile is detected as it rises above the horizon. Trackers and computers then calculate its trajectory and its point of impact so that it can be intercepted by other missiles. Even if new developments make such stations out of date for defence purposes they may continue usefully as space observatories with great possibilities.

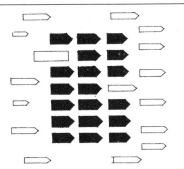

◄ Naval convoy—a quite different kind of covering force—is to protect merchant ships carrying vital food and supplies against enemy submarines and aircraft. Although packed close in the diagram, a real convoy is spread over kilometres of sea. The system was very much used by Britain against Germany in both World Wars.

◄ Blitzkrieg is German for 'lightning war', and was used by Hitler in 1939 and 1940. It means a surprise attack in overwhelming strength with columns of tanks overrunning the ground defences. While air-bombing paralyses the enemy rear, the tanks race ahead. Infantry 'mop up' any pockets of resistance.

◄ Azay-le-Rideau Castle, 16th century. More a fantasy than a fortification it was built as a residence for a financier, Gilles Berthelot.

►Deal Castle, one of Henry VIII's gun-forts, 1540. It consists of curving bastions, the inner higher than the outer, and the central keep highest of all, so that guns could be fired at different levels.

►Norman knight, with a mail hauberk reaching to his knees and a conical helmet with a 'nasal' which not only covered his nose but protected his whole face from a slashing blow. Far Right: German steel plate armour, 1520, was the best answer to arrows. The knight was covered from top to toe, but it weighed over 25 kg.

►Riot gear. In many countries the police have returned in recent years to the ancient protection of the shield. This is due to the increase in organized rioting, with the throwing not only of stones but of petrol bombs and other dangerous missiles.

Clothes and Fashion

► Roman couple wearing the basic costume of the Empire. She has a long straight dress with a cloak. He has a woollen toga folded and so skilfully draped over his tunic that it keeps in place without fastenings.

◄ Dutch nobleman wearing a short houpeland, 15th century. The houpeland was much favoured in the later Middle Ages. It was a very full garment with voluminous sleeves, 'dagged' at the edges. Some swept the ground. Ladies also took up the style. Note the open hood, worn like a cap, with a long slit point.

◄ German aristocrat and his wife, 1557. Both costumes closely follow Spanish fashion which was dominant in the 16th century. His padded hose is slashed to show the lining. The lady's gown is inspired by the Spanish *ropa*.

▼ Queen Elizabeth I and her courtier Sir Walter Raleigh were both noted for extravagant clothes —she wears a farthingale padded round the hips and an open ruff, while he has doublet, padded hose, and a ruff beneath his chin.

Fashion

One of the main motives for wearing clothes was vanity which soon led to dressing as a mark of rank. A man who wears a 'feather in his cap' appears taller and more self-confident. He soon adds more feathers, which causes rivalry with other feather-wearers. A fight follows, the winner (the chief) is allowed to wear the feathers. Still today it seems natural that an admiral should have more stripes on his sleeve than a captain. Men's clothes are influenced by the notion of rank.

By contrast, women's clothes are conditioned by sexual attraction. Different parts of the body at different times in different parts of the world have acquired a hidden charm and the fashionable clothes of the moment will uncover it or drape it or emphasize it in some other way. The veiling of the face in Islamic countries has an allure to the extent that if an Arab woman is surprised by a man without her veil she will raise her skirt instinctively to hide her face. Fashion can be described as exploiting these shifting zones of sex appeal.

In the earliest days the leaders of fashion were usually members of the royal court. They were the people with unlimited wealth, so that they could afford the finest materials, employ the best craftsmen, and collect more clothes than they ever had time to wear. When Queen Elizabeth I died she is said to have left 3000 dresses and 'head attires'. Far away in the depth of the countryside the bored ladies longed to

hear what was being worn in the capital. Farmers' wives questioned the travelling packmen and tried to get something new and different even if it was only a ribbon.

The 13th century Crusaders affected western fashions when they came back from the East with silks and muslins. Their wives and daughters soon adapted the oriental styles to suit themselves. The Muslim veil became the wimple, covering

▲ Mannequins display the designer's latest creations by parading on a raised 'cat-walk' before a selected audience of trade buyers, press and others. Here the clothes are by the Japanese designer, Kenzo.

From Trousers

Above: The vain Earl of Holland looks every inch a Cavalier during the Civil War, with lace even at his boot-tops. In fact, he soon joined the winning side, whose Puritan rule brought in an era of drab colours and plain styles as worn by the other figure shown. Above right: This lady wears a dress of richly painted linen, the man the elegant long coat and breeches of his class (France 1786). Right: Beau Brummell, 1788–1849, the rich Londoner who dictated men's dress fashions even to his royal friend, the Prince Regent.

To Mini skirt

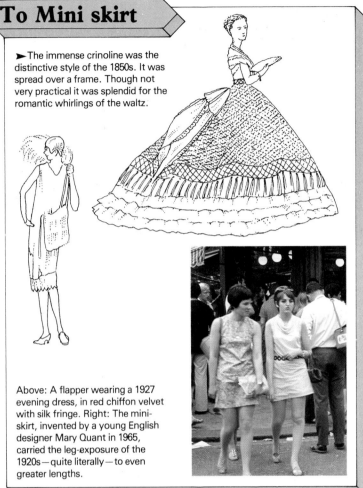

►The immense crinoline was the distinctive style of the 1850s. It was spread over a frame. Though not very practical it was splendid for the romantic whirlings of the waltz.

Above: A flapper wearing a 1927 evening dress, in red chiffon velvet with silk fringe. Right: The mini-skirt, invented by a young English designer Mary Quant in 1965, carried the leg-exposure of the 1920s—quite literally—to even greater lengths.

the lower part of the face. Sleeves became long and wide at the wrist.

In England the vogue for new materials was especially stimulated by Henry II's French wife, Eleanor of Aquitaine. She introduced wonderful silks interwoven with gold thread and embroidered designs from as far away as Iran and China.

In the main cities of medieval Europe the merchants were often far wealthier than the dukes and counts. They liked to show it by dressing themselves and their wives as magnificently as the nobility. Dick Whittington of London made so much money as a cloth merchant that he could lend Henry V £60,000 and burn the record of the debt.

A new technical invention can alter fashion. In 1856 came the first aniline dye, 'mauve', and there was a rapid swing to brighter colours from the former pastel shades. Even a best-selling novel can create a fashion—the 'Dolly Varden' dress took its name from the lively girl in Charles Dickens' *Barnaby Rudge.*

Fashion plates were first published in *The Lady's Magazine* of London in 1770. Every month, Marie Antoinette's dress designer sent dolls displaying her new styles to the cities of Europe.

The era of great designers dawned in 1858, when an Englishman, C. F. Worth, opened a salon in Paris and won the patronage of the Empress Eugénie. He it was who first adopted a haughty attitude to his wealthy customers, which only made them beg more humbly for his services.

Today there are many famous designers in Paris, London and Italy. Their 'shows' are attended by press and television teams. The latest styles are big news, flashed instantly across the world, adapted for mass production, and rushed into the shops. Fashion is no longer for the few. Despite the world's poverty, it is of interest to millions of ordinary people.

▼ In the prosperous 1960s, when jobs were plentiful, the young 'hippy' who disdained steady work sought to show his independence by his appearance. He was unemployed—and he looked it (left). The tough conditions of the 1980s brought high unemployment. Many keen, intelligent young people sought vainly for work. They found it important to keep up a smart and tidy appearance and this was mimicked by fashion (right).

Making

▶ Cro-Magnon antler needle, 40,000 BC. They threaded it with animal sinew. Metal needles came with the Bronze Age, in about 3000 BC.

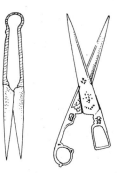

▲ Scissors have been known at least since the Romans. Left: 17th century type with spring. Right: Highly decorated Persian pair.

▼ Spinning wheel, 1480. With her left hand the woman pulled the yarn from the distaff. The right hand was used to turn the wheel.

▲ Singer's New Family sewing machine 1865. Within 20 years it was in more than 4 million homes, ending the drudgery of hand-sewing.

▼ Power-driven looms in the modern textile mill make cheap cloth available world-wide.

Washing

▲ American wash board, 1910, with an aluminium-coated rubbing surface of steel.

▼ Box mangle had a 'box' filled with heavy stones and rolled backwards and forwards over the damp laundry. Mangles have been used for drying newly-washed clothes since at least the 18th century.

▶ Washing machines sound modern—this one was made soon after 1850, but of course it was worked by hand and was not connected to the water-main. Thomas Bradford's machine had a rotating drum and included a vertical mangle.

▲ Very different is the washing machine of today. Plugged into the main electricity and water supply, and adjustable to the special requirements of different fabrics, it can be switched on and left by itself to do what once meant many hours of hot, exhausting labour.

Ironing

▶ Box iron 1840. Hot irons have been used for centuries—this one is only 6 cm long. The 'box' was a cavity to hold a chunk of very hot iron.

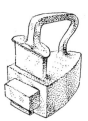

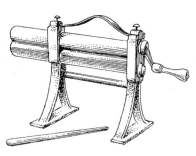

▲ Fluter, 1870. A special type of iron was used for pleats. It looked like a mangle but the rollers were of brass, heated by the insertion of red hot poker-shaped rods.

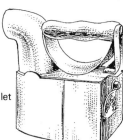

▶ A charcoal-heated iron, with chimney to let out the fumes.

▼ When gas became a popular heating agent it was applied to the iron. This one had a tube attached to the gas supply and a burner inside, pointed at the base.

▶ Electric iron, 1891. Soon electricity was competing with gas.

Clothes

Clothing began as protection. Later ideas of decency and fashion appeared.

Cavemen wore furs and animal skins. In hot lands they might use broad leaves and to this day grass skirts are worn on Pacific islands. To make cloth, though, men had to learn how to spin thread and weave different threads criss-cross into a piece of material.

No one knows who first invented spinning and weaving. Some people used wool or goat's hair. Others used the fibres of the cotton-plant or of flax (which makes linen) or the cocoon of the silk-worm. One of the most extraordinary materials used for making clothes was silk. Moth caterpillars often spin cocoons in which they change into moths. Silk thread comes from the cocoon of one kind of moth caterpillar. It is called a silk worm. The silk thread is carefully unwound from the cocoon on to a reel. The yarn made from it is woven into silk cloth. The Chinese were spinning silk about 3000 BC and at the same date, the Egyptians were exporting fine linen to other countries.

Spinning was mostly done by women. The fibres—wool or whatever—were cleaned, combed out of their tangle, and put on a distaff, a stick held under the left arm. With a spiral twist of her right hand the woman joined up the various loose ends and then, with a spindle dangling over that same right hand and literally 'spinning', she drew a continuous thread or yarn off the material on her distaff.

Until the 18th century, yarn spinning was done mostly by women at home. That is why we speak of 'homespun' and an unmarried woman is still sometimes called a 'spinster'. Weaving was more often done by men, who collected the yarn

▼ The most ancient method of washing clothes—in the cold running water of a river—can still be seen not only in India, as here on the bank of the Ganges, but in countless other places all over the world.

▲ The original sewing machine made in 1854 by the American, Isaac Merritt Singer (1811–1875). The idea of such a machine had occurred to an Englishman, Thomas Saint, in 1790, and a Frenchman, Thimmonier, invented a workable model in 1830. Eighty of his machines were installed in Paris, making army uniforms, but in 1841 they were wrecked by a mob and Thimmonier was nearly murdered. Several Americans then applied their minds to the project, and it was Singer who finally solved the technical difficulties and put his machine on the market.

from the cottages and wove it on looms at their own home or shed.

Then changes came. The spinning-wheel was invented and simplified the hand labour. In 1764 came the mechanical spinning jenny. Looms were improved and mechanized, so that weavers could keep pace with the extra yarn that was being spun.

In working-class families the women had always made most of the clothes. Only the well-to-do used tailors and dress-makers. Before they could even start cutting out and stitching, the women might have to dye the cloth themselves or bleach the linen, though in most towns there were tradesmen doing this work. Herbs and plants were used for the dyes and certain places became famous for particular colours. In the 13th century Robin Hood might have dressed his outlaws in Beverley blue or Stamford scarlet, but he sensibly put them into Lincoln green.

Now, by the early 19th century, the steam-powered mills of Britain were being quickly imitated in France, Germany and America, and cheap cloth was being exported all over the world. By 1854 the first Singer sewing machine had been invented and paper patterns were being printed. Women's and children's clothes, and men's shirts, could be made quickly and inexpensively in countless homes.

Factories were able to mass-produce suits and coats in every style, size and material. For the first time one could walk into a shop and buy ready-made clothes 'off the peg'. By the end of the 19th century these changes had put reasonable clothing within the means of all but the poorest people.

31

Top and Toe

Old people still remember when it was considered unsuitable to go outdoors without a hat or cap, even for children. Today, almost everyone goes bareheaded.

It is strange, because we lose a lot of body-heat through the uncovered head—and we give constant thought to 'insulation' in other ways. So why give up hats? It may be that they were a nuisance when getting into cars.

Headgear, of course, like other clothing, is not only for protection. It has always been a sign of wealth and dignity, a form of adornment—and a way to show respect. A man took off his hat to a lady, a boy raised his cap to his elders. They did the same when a funeral went by, or a royal procession, and always when entering a church.

Women on the other hand had to cover their heads in church, and only lately has this custom been relaxed. In a Jewish synagogue, men still cover their heads. Muslims also wear hats when worshipping and since the head touches the ground when praying, the flower-pot shaped fez developed without a brim.

In the past both sexes often kept their hats on indoors. It may have been partly because their homes were colder and draughtier than ours—but also because they felt more dignified. For centuries afterwards ladies wore large hats at the theatre (the programme used to request them to remove them, as people behind them could not see the stage). The diarist, John Croker, in 1828 complained that the large hats worn by his two companions at the dinner table resembled more umbrellas than hats and prevented him seeing his own plate. At formal luncheons to this day many ladies are still impressively behatted.

Hair-styles have varied just as much. Women have worn their hair long—or cut it short as in the 1920s, when the most extreme style was so boyish it was called the Eton crop. In the 18th century they piled it mountainously high, building it into structures so fantastic that ladies had to sleep sitting up. Once up, the hair stayed up, sometimes for months providing a perfect nest for insects! In the 19th century they pulled it back severely into the Victorian 'bun'. Curls and wavy hair have taken many ingenious forms. At one time they were only for the wealthy, with their maids and their exclusive hairdressers, but 20th century hair salons have put such services within the reach of all. Permanent waving was started in America by a German, Karl Nessler, developing it out of the 'Marcel waving' he had learnt from a Parisian, Marcel Grateau. It became hugely popular from 1915 onwards, when shorter hair became more practical in the wartime conditions and 'perming' was a way of 'prettying' it up.

Men have changed hair-styles less often, though they have always argued as to whether it should be long or short. During the 17th and 18th centuries the rich wore wigs, keeping their

Headwear

1. Black silk top hat, 1930. 2. Cloth cap, 1935. 3. Panama, 1935. 4. French beret, 1930.

◄ 5. Assyrian king's white felt tiara with bands of embroidery and pearls, 8th c. BC. 6. Turkish *taj* made with folds of white silk for a high-ranking official, 16th c. 7. French roundlet with chaperon and liripipe, early 15th c. 8. French triple-horned hennin made from brocaded silk with a gauze wimple, early 15th c.

Hairstyles

▲ Cypriote curls made from a toupée of rolls. Rome AD 86.

▲ Centre parting and strings of pearls, French 1560s.

▲ Wired ringlets tied with gold, Spain 1650s.

▲ French queen's coiffure, 1777 and directoire coiffure à la Titus.

Shoes

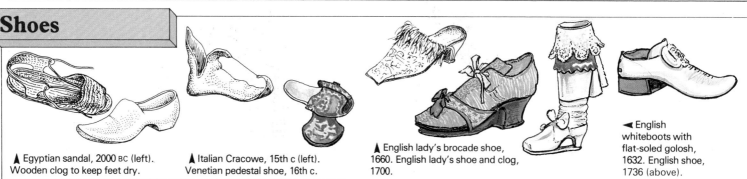

▲ Egyptian sandal, 2000 BC (left). Wooden clog to keep feet dry.

▲ Italian Cracowe, 15th c (left). Venetian pedestal shoe, 16th c.

▲ English lady's brocade shoe, 1660. English lady's shoe and clog, 1700.

◄ English whiteboots with flat-soled golosh, 1632. English shoe, 1736 (above).

own hair cropped short or even shaven. In 17th-century France, gentlemen going off to fight wore a 'campaign' wig (see below). In it they tied ribbons of different colours, known as 'favours'. These were tokens of love from the adoring women they had left behind.

People who care about dress like to be smart 'from top to toe', and shoes, beginning as protection, became in time a favourite means of display. From sandals of untanned hide or even plaited grass men progressed to proper leather shoes with a sole stitched to an upper, fastened with laces or thongs. Then the leather was brightly dyed. Velvet and silk were used, with gold and jewelled ornament. Humbler folk sometimes wore wooden clogs or sabots when working to keep their feet clean and dry. They were the ones who had to do the rough walking, and it was they who used heels long before the finer shoes had any. In the 14th century a fashion for men's shoes started in Cracow which spread all over Europe. Shoes were made with long points stuffed and wired to shape. A law was passed in 1363 regulating the length of the points of shoes: aristocrats were limited to 24 inch points (60 cms), gentlemen to 12 inch points (30 cms) and commoners to 6 inch points (15 cms)!

All footwear was made by hand until machinery was invented, in about 1810, to join sole and upper without hand-stitching. This meant cheaper boots for working people, though it was another hundred years before the barefoot child vanished from the London streets. Rubber came in, and its waterproof quality was made good use of—for galoshes in 1824, boots in 1865, separate heels in 1889. Since then, various synthetic materials have become substitutes for leather.

▲ Today hat-making is big business and revolves around 'The Season' that elusive time from April to August when the glamorous go out to be seen. One of the great modern hatters who caters for this is David Shilling who believes that the hat should be a beautiful object as well as an essential part of an outfit. Many of his hats are hung on the wall to be admired when they are not on the owner's head.

▲ French felt hat and campaign wig 1670s.

▲ Left: English felt hat, 1786. Gainsborough hat, 1780s (right).

▼ French directoire 'Incroyable', 1795. Hair cut in dog's ears.

▲ French bonnet of corded rose silk, lace veil, 1806.

◄ Far left: French evening coiffure, 1832. Left: English evening coiffure, 1840. Right: French evening coiffure, 1916. Far right: French heart-shaped coiffure dressed over rolls, 1940.

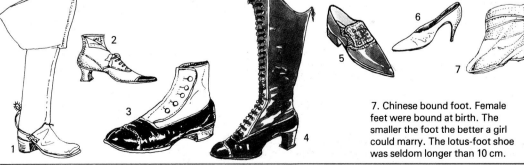

► 1. Military boot with a rigid leg to knee and wide top to cover lower thigh, c. 1705. 2. Woman's closed lace boot with patent cap, 1905. 3. Button balmoral with black patent golosh, 1914. 4. Black *glacé bal* leg boot with patent golosh, 1917. 5. Man's shoe, 1963. 6. The stiletto heel, 1958.

7. Chinese bound foot. Female feet were bound at birth. The smaller the foot the better a girl could marry. The lotus-foot shoe was seldom longer than 10 cm.

For Appearance's Sake

Originally, underwear was worn for warmth. Over the centuries, the purpose of underwear has changed. Roman women wore a long *tunica* under their outer garment, the *stola*. This feminine tunic became the smock or shift of the Middle Ages, the French *chemise*.

In 1600, a typical lady wore such a chemise, then a petticoat and a laced bodice stiffened with whalebone or even bands of iron, to give her a narrow waist and support her breasts. Another bodice went on the top of this, and a skirt or perhaps two skirts, before she put on her open-fronted gown. All these layers were meant to give her a stately appearance.

Seventeenth century underwear seems very full and bulky but ladies used to receive visitors dressed only in their underwear so it had to be. In those days a lady could have a revealing bosom while receiving a male visitor but if the calf of her leg was exposed a man with manners would hide his eyes as it was considered indecent.

▼ This painting of a woman by Rogier van der Weyden shows that make-up in 1433 emphasized the severe aspect of the face. The head was shaved to bring the hairline back, eyebrows were plucked, and the whole face was covered with very pale powder. Notice also the lack of jewellery. This sparse use of make-up is in contrast to the 18th century, when many ladies died as a result of using make-up containing poisonous white lead.

Drawers were a masculine garment. Women took to them only in about 1800, at first for riding. An advertisement in 1811 announced 'hunting drawers in elastic Indian cotton'.

The number of petticoats varied with fashion. In 1807, when dresses were very close fitting, an elegant lady wore just one thin petticoat, or none at all. But sixty years later even a child might have worn three, two white and one of coloured flannel, as well as frilly drawers and a chemise. Today, when so many dresses are made from light fabrics, a petticoat is often worn for modesty's sake.

By 1850, though, a development began in schools that was eventually to affect the dress of both sexes. It was the cult of organized sport, which soon swept the world.

Boys playing football or running races still wore underclothes, but they soon wanted briefer vests and 'pants' as they became known in Britain. Next, the heavier top garments were discarded leaving the underwear. The running vest, football jersey and shorts ('long' compared with today's) evolved from the lighter underwear and became, for sport, the only wear.

Having once discovered the advantages of the lighter underwear, however, men adopted it more and more for everyday purposes, under their suits and shirts—though it took a generation or two to convert the old-fashioned ones.

Women made similar changes for the same reasons, evolving their own clothes for exercise which led to lighter underwear for daily wear. 'Knickers' by 1900 had become a word for a feminine garment rather than a masculine one, as before. The brassière ('bra') was originally worn in the 1920s to flatten and conceal the breasts, giving a girl the boyish look that was then fashionable, but before long it was adapted to produce exactly the opposite effect. Synthetic materials were invented to take the place of wool and silk. Nylon stockings launched in the United States in 1940, were sold in Europe after World War II to replace the silk stockings that had covered ladies' legs for centuries. The most recent changes in underwear are the adoption of tights in place of stockings and the suspender-belts that had gone with them, and the removal of underwear altogether.

Make-up has altered much less. In ancient Rome a lady had beauty-aids still familiar today: pots of creams and colourings, scent-bottles, scissors, nail-files, tweezers, combs and hand-mirrors. There have really been only two fundamental changes.

First, mass-production and alluring advertisements have spread the use of cosmetics to the whole population. Secondly, scientific research and government regulations have largely got rid of the terrible health hazards of bygone days. Sixteenth-century ladies whitened their skin with ceruse, a horrifying mixture of white lead and vinegar, which withered the skin and could cause paralysis. They might redden their cheeks with mercuric sulphide, which ate into the flesh and finally destroyed it.

Jewellery too remains basically the same. Styles may vary and craftsmanship develop, but the necklace and brooch, the bracelet and the ring, keep their individual functions and recur in every century. The jewellery of 3000 years ago can be as breathtaking in its beauty as any piece created today. Fashions alter but come round again. In recent years some people have made fun of the punk with his earring. It is nothing new. The dandies of the 17th century had practised the same fashion—and long before them it had been all the rage in ancient Athens.

Make-Up

► Facial decoration is not confined to make-up. Tattooing is common among Polynesian tribes and is a mark of rank.

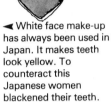

◄ White face make-up has always been used in Japan. It makes teeth look yellow. To counteract this Japanese women blackened their teeth.

► Indian make-up was and is used to emphasize the eyes. Note the heavy eyeliner and blackened eyebrows.

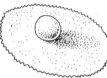

▲ Patching in 1650 grew to ludicrous proportions. Even men, known as *macaronis*, wore them.

Above right: Powder ball made from French chalk, and chamois leather for powdering the face, 1880. Right: Hand mirrors became indispensable for make-up after the mirror-silvering process was perfected in Venice in the 1320s.

◄ Even eyelashes went over the top in the 1960s (above). These are false with rhinestones.

▼ Stage make-up has been used for centuries to help establish a character.

Jewellery

◄ Neolithic marriage shell necklace, 15,000 BC. The rarer the object the better the bride.

▼ Chinese jade funerary pendant, 3rd c. BC.

▲ Disc-lipped women of the Kyabe tribe, Chad. Today this practice is illegal and very few of such women remain.

► Persian gold armlet with griffins, 5th c. BC (right).

▲ English memorial pendant, 1600. Especially fashionable after the execution of Charles I.

▲ Lyte jewel, 1610. Miniature of James I surrounded by 29 diamonds.

► Canning Jewel, Italian 16th c. A large baroque pearl mounted in enamelled gold, set with pearls, rubies and diamonds.

▼ English sapphire and diamond cluster necklace. The diamonds are from Brazil, 1860.

▼ 'Eye of Time' watch by Salvador Dali, of enamelled platinum set with diamonds and a ruby.

Underwear

► Corset of the Minoan snake goddess, 1900 BC. The breasts of Minoan women were bare.

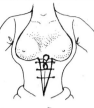

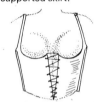

▲ 16th century corset, made of light steel plates to give a 13 inch (33 cm) waist!

▲ *Corps Baleine* (whalebone) supported the bust, 1730. The lady could rest her arms on her supported skirt.

▲ Bodice type corset used to give a tight bodice, high waist and raised bosom, France 1803.

▲ This whalebone corset gives a tiny waist, full bust and hips, 1878.

▲ Left: Flapper girl wearing a steel corset and bandeau. Middle: elastic cross over bands on the hips and a softly padded bra epitomize underwear of 1956. Right: By the 1960s, underwear was almost non-existent.

► The garter belt holds up the stockings, and the garter—a more temporary method of support.

Leisure and Pleasure

Toys and Games

Young children have a great deal of free time. They also have a great deal of energy to burn off. Looking at Bruegel's famous picture we see that children four hundred years ago were playing many of the games we know today. Louis XIII of France, who became king at the age of 9 when his father was murdered in 1610, enjoyed many of the pastimes of modern children. We know this because his doctor listed all the king's amusements. He cut up paper, he had a clockwork pigeon. And with his friends he played at soldiers, hide-and-seek, guessing games, charades, blind-man's-buff, and prisoners' base, as well as cards and chess. One of his favourites was a Tyrolese dance which involved him and the young pages in kicking each other's bottoms. One suspects that nobody kicked the royal bottom too hard. Many of these games were already hundreds of years old.

The ancient Greeks had seesaws and swings. They played with hoops. In Homer's poem, the *Odyssey*, in about 800 BC, the Princess Nausicaa plays ball with her ladies—and the men who all want to marry Penelope play draughts while she makes up her mind. Knuckle-bones and marbles were very early playthings. On the far side of the world the Chinese were flying kites by 300 BC, if not before.

Except for draughts and the more complicated game of chess, board-games and table-games came rather later. The first mention of cards is in China in AD 969, and they do not seem to have arrived in the West much before 1300. The earliest printed cards were made in Provence, France in about 1440, with the four suits and the court cards we have today. They were soon being produced in England too and in 1463 there was a ban on importing them from abroad.

One of the earliest card-games was probably piquet, for which you left out all the low-value cards, two to six. There were many different games in the 16th and 17th centuries, of which two have lasted, whist (originally 'whisk') and cribbage. Two other indoor games (not card-games) came in about the

▼ Children's Games by Pieter Bruegel, 1560. About 80 different games are depicted including leap frog, bowls, bumps, tag, follow-my-leader, spinning a top, rolling a hoop, stilts, a hobby horse, and marbles.

Toys

► Greek terracotta dolls, 5th c. BC. The arms and legs are secured to the body with metal pins. The doll is probably mankind's oldest toy. The first dolls were flat pieces of wood. Today's dolls talk and walk and even wet their pants!

▲ Pre-Columbian clay dog on wheels from an early Mexican culture.

▲ Bowling a hoop goes back to the earliest times. The first hoops were made from twisted reeds.

▲ Rattle, 1570. It has an ivory teething stick at one end and a whistle at the other.

▲ Among the simplest of toys is the cup and ball game. This one is made from turned wood, 19th c.

▲ Left: The Napoleonic Wars boosted interest in toy soldiers. This one is made of wood, 1800. Middle left: Talking picture blocks, 1890s. Middle right: Teddy bear 1910. Right: Toy Mercedes 28/32, 1908.

▲ One of the earliest electric trains. A Bing steeple locomotive and carriage in gauge 3.

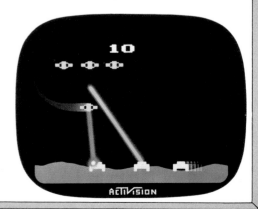
►Space invaders game, 1980s. In many ancient cultures one of the first things taught to the young was the use of weapons.

same period, billiards, and backgammon—using draughtsmen and dice.

Bridge did not arrive until the early 20th century. For children, however, manufacturers began to produce all kinds of board-games—halma (1890), ludo (1898) and an endless variety of racing games with dice and counters. The most popular of all was, and is, Monopoly, invented by an unemployed American engineer and launched at Christmas, 1935. It swept the world, selling millions of sets.

Toys have as long a history as games. The baby's rattle is said to have been invented by the Greek philosopher, Archytas, Plato's friend. He gave rattles to the children of his slaves, saying that if young people could not make a noise they would wreck the house. Probably, though, the rattle is even more ancient. When it seemed too babyish, older children soon equipped themselves with toy drums and trumpets.

Toy animals appeared early. In what is now Iran children in 1100 BC were pulling lions and porcupines on wheels. Children will always have dolls, even if the doll is no more than a bit of wood or cloth and a lot of imagination. Like most things, the doll has changed down the ages, becoming more and more beautiful and lifelike. The first recorded dolls' house was made for the Duke of Saxony's daughter in 1558, but this was really more of an expensive model—the dolls' house as a toy to play with did not arrive until about 1700.

Meanwhile, Louis XIV played with soldiers, so did the future Tsar Peter III, and countless other famous men to be, including Winston Churchill and H. G. Wells. At first the soldiers were flat, then in about 1870 they were made in the round, mostly in Germany where the toy trade had been centred since the first carved wooden toys were marketed in the 15th century. In 1893 an Englishman began making lead soldiers that were hollow-cast by a secret method which made them much cheaper to produce, and this type dominated the market until plastic figures came in.

Toy trains soon followed the invention of the real ones, then toy cars and aeroplanes—and of course all kinds of constructional toys and working models. The most modern toys are electronic and computer games but these do not hold the interest for long periods and sales of building bricks, wooden toys and jigsaws have not decreased significantly.

The Teddy Bear

Toys often responded to news and the latest fashions, and as there is big money now in toy-manufacture there is a constant struggle to sell the public something fresh. The teddy bear came in 1903, so-called because a real-life bear cub was saved by Teddy Roosevelt, the US President on a hunting-trip, and within a short time the German manufacturers were exporting a million a year. When the first giant panda arrived in a western zoo, in 1936, it was not long before the shops were selling cuddly replicas. And when space-travel began, every small boy had to have a spaceship and an astronaut's outfit.

Appearances and fashions alter, but toys and games still cater for the same basic instincts of children—aggressive, competitive, protective, comforting or the urge to solve a problem. Ernest Froebel was one of the first teachers to realize their educational value. He opened a school in Germany in 1837 called a *kindergarten* (childgarden) where he used toys to teach the children.

Playing Cards

▲ Marseilles Tarot 'Death', 15th c.

▲ Marseilles Tarot 'Lovers', 15th c.

▲ Le Comte de Toulouse, French, 16th c.

▲ 7 of Animals, French 1650.

▲ Geographical pack—Jack of Spades, Italy 1670.

▲ Early Italian pack—6 of *spade* (swords).

▲ Minchiate pack—The Twins Trump 35, Italy 1790.

▲ Tarot—Trump 17, German 1800.

▲ 'Le Feu de Blocus' pack commemorating Napoleonic Wars.

▲ Tarot Trump 19, Austrian 1830.

▲ Stories from German literature pack—7 diamonds, 1839.

▲ German theatrical pack—King of Diamonds: the actor Beeker, 1840.

▲ King of Spades, English 1880.

▲ Austrian pack for Jubilee of Emperor Franz Josef, 1900.

▲ German pack to acclaim war effort—Ober of Leaves, 1917.

▲ Belgian pack with deaf and dumb inserts, 1970s.

Sport

The first sportsmen and women we know about were the Greeks. Their Olympic Games were founded in 776 BC and held every four years until AD 393, 1169 years in all, a record as remarkable as any set up by the athletes themselves. Our modern Olympics are a revival. They started at Athens in 1896 and have been held in different countries ever since.

The Greek love of sport was even older than the Games. We read of the legendary Argonauts boxing with rawhide gloves. And that other hero, the wily Odysseus, won a boxing contest for which the prize was a pudding. In later years the Greek boys were taught these poems and stories and were taught also that the gymnasium was an essential part of a balanced education. The Greeks were the first people to have sporting heroes—when Olympic winners went back to their own cities they were given a tremendous welcome, and famous poets wrote odes in their honour.

Athletics, horse-races and chariot-races were what they liked. They seem not to have gone in for team-games, though something very like hockey is depicted in one of their sculptures. The Romans, when they conquered Greece, kept up the Olympics and the chariot-racing continued as a popular spectacle in their eastern capital, Byzantium. In fact, it was spectacle more than sport that the Romans preferred—we can tell that from their bloodthirsty love of fights between gladiators or wild animals in the arena.

Ball-games came later.

Football, the popular favourite, was played in medieval England. A monk wrote that it was 'abominable' and 'more common, undignified and worthless than any other kind of game'. He mentioned a youth who, 'being struck in his most sensitive parts by the foot of one who played with him, sustained long and intolerable pains.' The youth survived, however—and so did football. Then came a day in 1823 destined to be a landmark in sporting history. As a memorial tablet at Rugby School records a boy named William Webb Ellis 'with a fine disregard for the rules of football as played in his time, first took the ball in his arms and ran with it.'

That was the beginning of Rugby football, handling the ball, as distinct from 'soccer', so called from the Football Association founded in 1863. The first of its clubs, Notts. County, had been founded the previous year. 'Soccer' became more and more a professional sport, a mass spectacle entertaining vast crowds. 'Rugger' remained primarily amateur, but with an off-shoot organization of professionals with somewhat different rules. Both games have spread to many other countries.

Cricket began in England and was played all over the British Empire in the 19th century. It is still played in many of those countries and played brilliantly, particularly in India, Pakistan, Sri Lanka, West Indies, Australia, New Zealand

Track and Field

▲ Greek girl winning race at the women's Olympics at Hera.

◄ Sumo wrestling in Japan dates from 1624 and is still practised today.

► Hunters on skis from Lapland, 1539. Today shooting and skiing is represented by an Olympic sport—the biathlon.

Ball Games

▲ Greek game of 'hockey'.

▲ Mayan ball game. You had to hit the ball through the hole using knee, hip or elbow!

▼ Playing bowls, 1640. Earlier, King Richard II had banned bowls fearing that it might jeopardize the practice of archery.

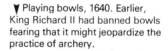

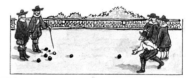

▲ Preparing a football by blowing up a leather-cased pig's bladder, 1600.

Animal Sport

◄ Bull-leaping, Crete 1900 BC. Teams of three men and women somersaulted between the horns of a charging bull.

► Gladiators fighting starving lions was a popular sport in Rome, AD 60. Gladiators were usually slaves or criminals.

▲ Chariot racing, Constantinople AD 500. Different political parties raced against each other. The losing party often caused a riot.

and South Africa. The name comes from *cricc*, or crook, and the game started in Saxon times as a diversion for bored shepherds, defending the wicket gate of their sheep-pen from an improvised ball. The curved wood continued until about 1770, when the straight bat was adopted to cope with more accurate bowling. The MCC (Marylebone Cricket Club) was founded in 1787 and still controls the sport—its London ground, Lord's, was laid out by Thomas Lord in 1814.

Tennis was forbidden as 'dangerous' at Narbonne College in France in 1379. But the modern form, lawn tennis, dates only from 1875, when rules were drawn up for a game to be played on grass instead of in expensive covered 'courts'. The famous Wimbledon championship started only two years afterwards and the new game swiftly gained world-wide popularity, marked by the Davis Cup donated in 1900.

Golf was born in Scotland. It was banned there as early as 1457—often the first date we know for a sport is the year some one disapproved of it!—but a century later it was played by Mary Queen of Scots herself. Her son took it south when he became James I of England, but it long remained a Scottish game. The first tournament was held in 1744, the first 18-hole course laid out at St Andrews in 1764.

There is no space to mention all the sports. The ancient game of hockey, still widely played, has acquired a new speed and excitement since played on ice in Canada in 1875. Baseball, America's own special game, developed from the children's game of rounders, was first played in 1845. And the

sedate, innocent-looking but very crafty game of bowls, banned (needless to say) under Richard II in 1388 but played by Drake while waiting for the Spanish Armada precisely 200 years later, is still a most popular and sociable pastime. So, in France, is its equivalent *boule*, played with devout concentration usually not on trim lawns but on the hard-trodden earth under the plane-trees on some small-town boulevard.

▼ The Grand National. This race course has some of the largest fences in the world, some are over 2 metres high. The result is that many horses fall throwing their jockeys.

▲ Boxing is another old sport. Prize fighting started in London i the 18th century. The fighters wore no gloves.

▲ Left: Woman throwing the discus. Right: Jesse Owens wins the long jump with a leap of 8.06 m at the 1936 Olympics.

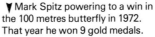
➤ Susan Tiedke the East German gymnast performing on the assymetrical bars.

▼ Mark Spitz powering to a win in the 100 metres butterfly in 1972. That year he won 9 gold medals.

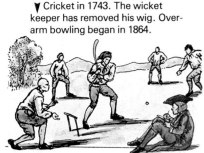
▼ Cricket in 1743. The wicket keeper has removed his wig. Over-arm bowling began in 1864.

▲ Women playing tennis at Wimbledon in the 1880s.

▲ Pelota is a very fast game that originated in northern Spain.

➤ American baseball.

▲ Jousting, 1400. To train for war, knights fought in mock battles.

▼ Bear baiting, 16th c.

▲ Hunting the hare was a sport for gentlemen, 16th c.

▲ Hawking, 1600, was popular all over Europe.

The Changing Theatre

▲ Greek drama developed from dances performed on a flat area levelled off on the slope of a hill from where the audience watched, 8th c. BC.

▲ A Greek theatre, 5th c. BC. Performances lasted all day, consisted of three full length plays and ended with a farce so everyone went home happy.

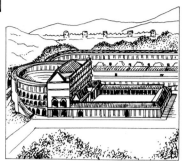

▲ Roman theatre at Orange, France. Because of the distance to the stage, actors wore large masks to show the character played by the actor.

▲ Chinese theatre during a festival in the 12th century AD. At the end of the play a rhyme summed up the story. One of the lines was the title of the piece.

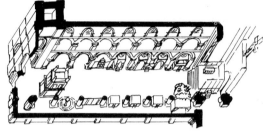

▲ An important development in western drama was the acting of plays in churches. Religious scenes were then played in different parts of the church where special stages called mansions had been set up. Each one represented a place—Galilee, Paradise, Hell and so on.

Religious plays were performed at pageants (left). Passion plays (above) told the story of Jesus, and took as long as 25 days to perform.

▲ Shakespeare's Globe theatre. The stage was on two levels. On the day of performance a flag flew all day. The second gallery had the most comfortable seats '. . . where he not only sees well, but can also be seen'.

▲ Kabuki theatre dates back to 1586 and remains the main form of drama in Japan. The stage is always the same shape, the most striking feature of which is the *hanamichi*—a causeway that runs through the audience.

▶ Theatre built by Cardinal Richelieu in 1641. Note the proscenium arch stage—one of the first. It replaced the openness of Shakespeare's theatre. Not only the stage had changed, drama was now exclusive to the court and pandered to it. Molière later made this theatre famous.

▲ A pantomime at the Haymarket theatre, 1790s (above left). Pantomime dates back to Roman times when mythological stories were mimed. By the 18th century actor managers like John Rich had combined the myth with a story from the *commedia dell'Arte* with Harlequin and Columbine the central characters. A beautiful example of German baroque (above right) in the Cuvilliers Theatre in Munich. Note the proscenium arch and the tiers of boxes.

▲ The Penthouse theatre, in Washington, Seattle is a theatre-in-the-round, which attempts to make the theatre less formal.

Stagecraft

▲ *Commedia dell'Arte* was popular mime and improvisation, Italian 16th c. The main characters were Gilles, Columbine and Harlequin.

▲ Molière's *Comédie Française* developed from the Italian *commedia dell'Arte*, 1680s. Here are Gilotin and Guillot Gorju two of the many characters that always appear.

▲ David Garrick as Macbeth and Mrs. Pritchard as Lady Macbeth, 1746. In the 18th century contemporary costume was worn. Garrick is dressed as an army officer!

➤ Star trap in operation, 1893. Mainly used in farces and ghost scenes, it caused many accidents.

▲ A horserace with real horses on stage at the Union Square Theater, New York, with moving panorama and treadmills run by electric motors, the speed of which was controlled by the man on the right, 1890.

➤ Backstage at a theatre showing scene changes, flyweights, lighting box and wing lighting, 1880.

The Theatre

It is not certain when the drama of the Far East began, but it had been flourishing for centuries when a Chinese emperor founded the world's first official drama school, the Pear Garden, in AD 20. And 13 plays by the Indian writer, Bhasa, have come down to us from the 3rd century BC.

In the West we have more definite records. Drama there began with the Greeks and we can still see the ruins of their vast open-air theatres. As in China, plays in Greece developed out of religious festivals with teams of dancers. The next step was to have an actor who told a story by holding a dialogue, between dances, with the leader of the chorus.

Aeschylus, who lived from about 525 to 456 BC, is the first known playwright. He acted himself, trained the dancers, and directed the whole performance. He had the idea that it would make all the difference to have a second actor, so that the story could be acted more vividly, not just told in long speeches. He also introduced scenery.

Athens held annual drama festivals with prizes for the best plays. Aeschylus had a brilliant rival, Sophocles. Sophocles thought, why not a third actor? He wrote one into his plays, and then Aeschylus did the same. Sophocles thought, why not better scenery. So that came in too.

These two writers of tragedies, together with another, Euripides, and a writer of comedies, Aristophanes, raised drama to a standard of excellence. Between them they wrote well over 300 plays, but as printing was not invented then only 42 have come down to us. They still compare well with anything written since, and stand production on television.

We might say, in fact, that drama did not change much for nearly 2000 years after them. The Romans had theatres, drama continued with strolling players, or workmen acting in the streets on Christian holy days, but the theatre really began to change in Italy during the Renaissance in the 16th century when the old Greek plays were rediscovered.

After this all kinds of dramatic entertainment developed, the essential being to amuse the audience. This audience was sometimes cultured and courtly, sometimes uneducated and 'popular'. Poetic tragedy and comedy, melodrama and broad farce, music and spectacle, had each its following. The actor became as important as the writer—Shakespeare and Molière were both. The introduction of actresses in the 16th century (17th in England) opened a new epoch.

The actor's standing in society depends on the role of the theatre in that society. In very primitive societies the actor is an asset, a talent to amuse making him a centre of the community. In a sophisticated society where he is paid for his services he may be the object of adulation and envy to some and scorned by others who feel it improper to reward someone for any form of pretence. Thus Plato thought actors worthless hypocrites. Aristotle believed them to be worth looking after and the modern Russian government pays them a salary and a pension. In the west they are more independent and have risen from their old status of 'rogues and vagabonds' to their modern respectability. When Queen Victoria knighted Henry Irving in 1895, it was a milestone. It is interesting to note that no society could tolerate a lady actor until the late 16th century. But today the actress has as much respect as the actor—one of the few professions where that is true.

From Pipe to Pop

There is hardly a period in history or a race of people that cannot boast some sort of musical tradition, some conscious moulding of random sound into an artistic form, whether it be the shepherd's pipe sounding in the hills thousands of years ago, or the thunder of a hundred-piece symphony orchestra in a modern concert hall. But there is a tendency to see all music as a steady crescendo reaching its climax with Western music. This is misleading, the music of the Far East, or the African pigmy and the Australian aborigine for that matter have their own quite different forms worthy of respect.

The first musical instruments developed out of implements that had other uses—the stringed instrument from a hunter's bow, the drum from an upturned pot, the rattle from a seed drill. The instruments also depended on materials available and lifestyle—shepherds had pipes—they had time to make them, nomads had small easily-portable instruments and so on. Some early instruments were: the Jew's harp, a simple drum, pan pipes and bagpipes.

The Assyrian king, Assurbanipal, had quite an orchestra, with pipes, harps and drums, in the 7th century BC. Music was important, too, in the theatres and schools of ancient Greece. Yet those bygone civilizations, so advanced in many ways, never thought of the fiddler's bow.

That came much later with the Arabs, the source of so many new ideas. They devised a pear-shaped, stringed instrument, played with a bow and called a *rebab*. It first reached Europe in the 9th century and was the ancestor of the violin.

Before that, in about AD 700, Italian monks had written their choral music with lines to show the rise and fall of the voice. This was the beginning of the musical notation that is used today. But the church considered musical instruments other than the organ and the human voice to be pagan, and the development of music away from choral music was largely secular.

➤ Phineas T. Barnum started his first circus in 1871, having previously toured with a 'museum' showing the celebrated 'General Tom Thumb'—the smallest man alive. His circuses were famous for their razzmatazz and extraordinary animal acts featuring lions, tigers and elephants. Barnum died in 1891, requesting with his last words the day's receipts of the circus.

The Circus

▼ 'Daring Young Men on the Flying Trapeze'—the kings of the circus.

▲ German circus 1640.

▲ Astleys 60 foot (18 m) amphitheatre established the size of the circus ring, 1777.

▲ The Holborn Amphitheatre's permanent ring had coconut matting instead of sawdust, 1870.

Music

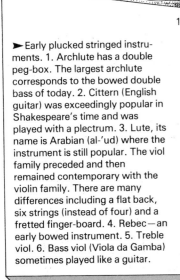

The violin family—7. Violin. 8. Viola. 9. Violoncello ('cello). 10. Double bass. Left: The octobass was 3 m high. It was invented by J. B. Vuillaume (1850) at Berlioz' suggestion. As the finger-board was above the head of the player, 'stopping' was done using foot and hand levers. Below right: Roman brass trumpets from Trajan's column in Rome.

➤ Early plucked stringed instruments. 1. Archlute has a double peg-box. The largest archlute corresponds to the bowed double bass of today. 2. Cittern (English guitar) was exceedingly popular in Shakespeare's time and was played with a plectrum. 3. Lute, its name is Arabian (al-'ud) where the instrument is still popular. The viol family preceded and then remained contemporary with the violin family. There are many differences including a flat back, six strings (instead of four) and a fretted finger-board. 4. Rebec—an early bowed instrument. 5. Treble viol. 6. Bass viol (Viola da Gamba) sometimes played like a guitar.

Ordinary folk sang carols, folk-songs and ballads. Troubadours toured Europe singing love songs in the castle halls. There was music for dancing and for grand processions. In Shakespeare's England everyone was expected to be able to sing or to play an instrument. In barbers' shops there might be a lute or cittern (see below) for the use of waiting customers, as newspapers are today. And musicians were beginning to play together in harmony. The 'orchestra' was evolving. In the 16th century it was just a consort of stringed instruments varied only by a flute. Brass instruments were added in the 1600s, and so the orchestra grew by degrees, especially as old instruments like the flute were improved and new ones like the clarinet (about 1690) were invented. Mozart (1756–1791) was delighted when he discovered the clarinet's wonderful range and power, and in his *Paris* Symphony he gave the wind instruments equal importance with the strings.

The 18th century was one of immense progress in music. The first piano was made in 1709. Haydn (1732–1809), called 'the father of the symphony', achieved a mastery of wind instruments in his compositions. J. S. Bach (1685–1750) made revolutionary improvements in the organ and influenced music in many other ways. And the 19th century maintained the impetus of change. Mozart's orchestra of 35 to 40 players rose to Wagner's and Richard Strauss's 100 or more players.

Until 1672 the only way to hear a fine orchestral concert was as guest of some prince who could maintain his own musicians. There were no ordinary public concerts until John Banister, the leader of Charles II's court musicians, was dismissed for impertinence to the King and started to give performances in a room in a London ale-house. This was a real landmark in musical history, though it was twenty-five years before any other country followed the English lead and held a public concert, but when they did it was not in an ale-house.

Besides 'classical' music there are all the popular songs, dance-tunes and other types, which give pleasure to millions and have sometimes influenced the great composers. Dances like the minuet and the waltz are examples of this. Later still, jazz, which started in New Orleans about 1900, and has been marked by brilliant improvization and superb technical mastery, has had an effect in other fields of music. A quite different development was 'pop' music, starting with an American group, the Bluecaps from Nashville (1956), soon to be overshadowed by Elvis Presley and The Beatles from Liverpool, and others, catering for a new and enthusiastic public of high-earning teenagers. 'Pop' music was not to be confused with 'popular' music—the sentimental ballads, comic songs and other types—which had become widespread among the masses in the 19th century, as sheet-music and pianos entered so many homes.

Today electronics have brought a revolution of their own, with the microphone and electric guitar and now the Moog Synthesizer creating its own new sound.

◄ Clowns developed from the *zanni* of the Italian *commedia dell'Arte* in the 17th century. Left to right: Auriol, the fool, Gilles, Percy Huxter (white-faced clown), Coco (Auguste) and Little Billy (midget).

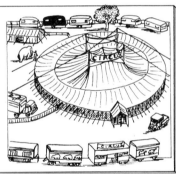

► The big top and surrounding buildings including the animal tents.

▲ Brass. 11. French military bugle. 12. Tuba. 13. The Natural Horn, with crooks. Crooks lengthened the tubing producing a different pitch.

Woodwind. 14. Recorder showing finger positions. 15. Piccolo (fife)—a member of the flute family, it gives the highest notes the orchestra possesses. 16. 19th century flageolet, a member of the recorder family. 17. Clarinet, a reed blown instrument. 18. Double bassoon—a member of the oboe family.

19. Early virginal: one string to one note—plucked. Similar to a spinet but smaller. Young ladies (hence the name) played it placed on a table. 20. Harpsichord: two or more strings to a note—plucked. 21. Upright grand piano. Hammers strike the strings. 22. Grand Piano. The piano was invented by Cristofori in Florence, 1709. Right: Atlanta city organ—the world's largest. Wind supplied by bellows blows a series of organ pipes which are like huge whistles.

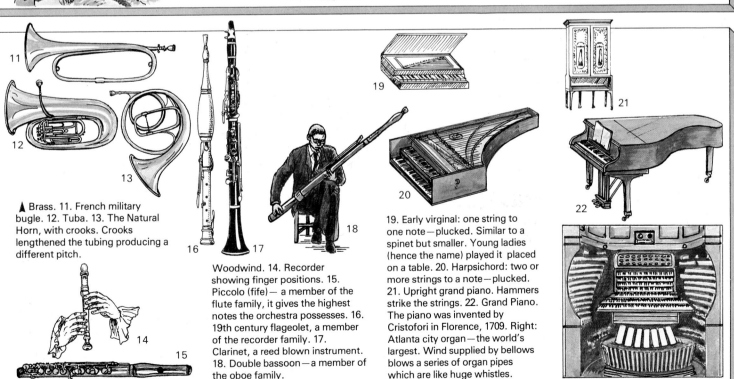

Magic of Painting

History of Western Painting

▲ Egyptian tomb painting, 1600 BC. How the foot is painted tells you most about how painting developed. The Egyptians painted people with two left feet, i.e. you can only see the big toes.

▲ Fresco from the Minoan palace at Knossos, 1400 BC. The servants are shown with a left and a right foot with all the toes marked.

Our oldest pictures are cave-paintings in France and Spain of reindeer and bison and other animals, skilfully outlined in clays stained with iron oxide—perhaps 18,000 years ago.

Much later, when men began building, a smooth wall gave them a better surface to paint on. They experimented with other substances and extended their choice of colours. Their subjects became more varied—they could show marching armies and charging chariots, gods and kings and fabulous creatures. Besides painting frescoes on flat walls they coloured their statues and 'reliefs'. Reliefs were the carved or moulded pictures that stood out from the wall but were not, like statues, separate and movable.

Another early form of picture-making did not need paint at all—it was the 'mosaic', made up like a jigsaw puzzle from countless bits of different coloured stone, set in cement. It was ideal for floors, because the colours did not fade.

The Greeks did most to set western art on the path of development it has followed to this day. Though their paintings have vanished their sculpture still shows the skill they achieved. In depicting the human body their artists had the advantage of being able to study the anatomy and muscle-movement of naked athletes.

After Europe became Christian, art became religious. The Catholic Church wanted mural paintings, statues and altar-pieces that would tell the Bible story and the lives of the saints. In the Arab countries art developed quite differently, because the Koran, the holy book of Islam, forbade the depiction of men and animals, so it was safer to stick to flowers and geometrical patterns. Much Oriental skill went into the design of woven rugs and carpets.

In the West the mosaics gradually went out of fashion, for they took much labour and were very costly. Frescoes were cheaper because they were quicker. A young Italian mosaic-worker named Giotto turned to frescoes, and in 1304—a landmark date in art history—he painted the walls of the Arena Chapel in Padua. The figures in his pictures had a new solidity which led eventually to an understanding of perspective—the method of giving depth to a picture by showing people and objects smaller at a distance, and of conveying the solidness of things. Giotto had opened a new chapter in painting.

Still no-one had discovered a way to fix and preserve the brightness of colours. This was done by two Flemish brothers, Jan and Hubert van Eyck. They mixed linseed oil with their paints and discovered oil painting. Now, instead of painting on plaster or wood, artists could paint on stretched canvas. The 'easel' picture, which could be moved and hung anywhere, was born. Subjects began to change. Art branched out.

Until the 19th century artists mostly took commissions from the church or from rich customers and produced the work they ordered. It was a major step forward when artists of the 19th century started to paint pictures for themselves. No longer restricted by the taste of non-artists, painters began to experiment. Between the 1850s and 1950s there was a painting revolution that created Impressionism, Cubism, Surrealism, Abstract Expressionism and Pop Art to name only a few of the many varied styles.

▲ Leonardo: *Virgin of the Rocks*, 1483. Leonardo's skill in engineering, poetry and sculpture, as well as in painting, makes him the true 'Renaissance Man'.

▲ Titian: *Portrait of a Man with a blue sleeve*, 1511. Titian was a Venetian. Venetian painters were famous for their use of light and colour.

▲ Turner: *Venice, calm at sunrise*, 1842. This beautiful watercolour is an impression rather than an accurate description of Venice. Above right: Courbet: *Funeral at Ornans*, 1849. Courbet believed in painting life as it was without glamorizing it. It was known as the Realist School. Right: Monet: *The Water-lily Pond*. He was the main founder of Impressionism—the theory that all light is colour.

▲ Soldier on Greek red-figure vase, 480 BC. For the first time a foot is drawn as seen from the front.

▲ Italian illuminated manuscript, c. 1490. In the early days of Christianity, every rich Christian owned a little bible richly illustrated. The tradition continued into the 16th century.

▲ Giotto: *Lamentation of the Dead Christ*; Arena Chapel, Padua, 1304–13.

▲ Jan van Eyck: *The Arnolfini Wedding*, 1434; National Gallery, London.

▲ Caravaggio: *The Supper at Emmaus*, 1596. He was the first person to use peasants and people off the street as models for his religious pictures. His paintings caused a scandal.

▲ Ingres: *Oedipus and the Sphinx*, 1827. Ingres was the champion of Neoclassicism (the harking back to Classical Greece for style and content) against Romanticism.

▲ Delacroix: *Jacob wrestling with the Angel* (detail, 1853). Romanticism stood for space, colour and life not the rigid formality of Neoclassicism which Delacroix opposed.

▲ Magritte: *The use of words* (This is not a pipe), 1929. One of the most important artists of the Surrealist movement. He tried to make us rethink the relationship between words and images. For instance, this is not a pipe, it is a picture of one. Left: Picasso: *Weeping Woman*, 1937. Picasso was the co-founder of Cubism in 1907, this picture still has Cubist characteristics. But more than this the picture transmits a feeling of bitterness and violence to a world on the brink of war.

▲ Rothko: *Light Red over Black*, 1957. Abstract movement. The red and black together create the feeling of vibration and vitality as effectively as any portrait or landscape.

The Hand of the Craftsman

'Arts and crafts' are often bracketed together, but there is an important distinction.

A skilled craftsman knows his materials, his tools and his techniques. He will make things to order, he will make six bowls or six chairs to match, and he may work out his own ideas and designs. But only if he has real originality can he rate as an artist in the full sense.

For originality—imagination—is the artist's essential quality. He needs technical mastery too, but imagination matters even more than manual skill. A painter of genius may be forgiven for a blemish of detail in expressing his vision. A craftsman has no excuse for faulty workmanship.

Craftsmen began with useful articles but the impulse to decorate them was always strong.

The original motives for decoration are so remote from our own that it requires a considerable leap of the imagination to understand them. Primitive people were consumed by fear not of tangible things like wild animals, floods and fire but by evil spirits and any markings made on themselves or on a bit of bone or on a sluice gate were to ward off these spirits and in effect were supposed to bring them good luck. Over the centuries these motives have changed, decoration has become a habit but the members of the community who are most successful at making the 'markings' have always been singled out. They are the craftsmen and in the second artistic wave the object to be decorated became as important as the decoration itself.

So far, the earliest ornament found is a 200,000 year old hand axe which has been shaped around the star-shaped fossil of a sea urchin. To the owner, this hand axe presumably had more power than his neighbour's without a pattern.

Early Crafts

Basket-making is certainly one of the earliest crafts to be developed. Neolithic workers coiled and plaited reeds much in the way that baskets are made today. But basket-making helped the development of other crafts. The plaiting of grass and rushes showed the way to the weaving of fibres into cloth. And when baskets had been smeared with clay to fill the gaps it was soon realised that a similar shape, made of clay alone, became a pot.

By 4000 BC the potter's wheel had been invented. At first this was two flat round slabs one more convex than the other. One person spun the slab, another shaped the clay. The foot-wheel operated by one person was not invented until about 200 BC. The principle of the potter's wheel inspired the woodworker's lathe, which the Greeks had by 1500 BC.

People learnt to make pots in more than one piece and join the pieces—a narrow neck or a handle—with wet clay. And in decorating some special item they learnt that the paints they applied had also the effect of making the pot more water-tight. So glazing and other processes were discovered, and were used for the workaday pots as well as the show pieces. Glazing in turn led to the making of glass which appeared simultaneously in Egypt and Mesopotamia in 1400 BC.

Woodwork, which really comprises a number of crafts, has evolved most since the Middle Ages, when (apart from splendid carvings) it was mainly a question of sound carpentry. Then, in the 16th century, the 'joiner' emerges with his finer techniques, and after about 1600 the 'cabinetmaker' appears, leading on to the great 18th-century furniture designers.

Guilds came with the Middle Ages when the craftsmen in each trade formed a guild to keep up standards and prevent unfair competition. A boy became apprentice to a master craftsman and was thoroughly trained, seven years being the usual period, during which he lived in his master's house. Then he could become a journeyman and receive proper wages. He could not set up on his own account until he had submitted a specimen of his workmanship (his 'master piece'). If the guild thought it good enough he was made a member and then he could employ assistants.

With the coming of factories, and cheap machine-made goods, many of these skilled master craftsmen could no longer earn a living. In many trades they gradually died out. Some special skills were completely lost as no fresh apprentices came to learn them. Then, in the middle of the 19th century, there was a reaction against the ugliness and sameness of some factory products. In England, the movement was led by William Morris, a writer who was also keenly interested in various crafts—printing and carpet-weaving and house-furnishing. In 1861 he helped to start a firm with higher artistic standards in this field, and his teaching had wide influence.

Today, mass-production is necessary to supply most every-day items but, as a reaction, similar to William Morris's, many craftsmen have returned to skills that were becoming extinct —working as coopers, saddlers, violin-makers, jewellers, thatchers and weavers.

▼ Egyptian peasant making a pot by the same method his ancestors would have used 2000 years ago.

Photography

▲ Portable *camera obscura*, 1694. An image of the landscape was projected on to paper ready for tracing.

▲ Silhouette, 1790. The profile was traced from the shadow cast by a lamp on to a piece of paper.

▲ Photograph by Niépce, 1827. A photo-sensitive pewter plate replaces the paper of the *camera obscura*.

▲ The first Daguerreo-type camera, 1839. Daguerre's process required a much shorter exposure time.

▲ Fox Talbot's picture of Lacock Abbey was made in 1843 using the Calotype process which he had invented in 1841. It was the first negative/positive process and meant that an infinite number of prints could be taken from one negative.

1   2   3   4

1. F. H. Powell's single-lens stereoscopic camera, 1858, produced 3-dimensional views when the developed photograph was seen through a special eyepiece. 2. The Stern detective camera was designed to be worn under a waistcoat with the lens poking through a button-hole, 1886. 3. Photographic studio, 1860. 4. In a portable dark tent, the professional photographer could process his plates on the spot. 5. Brownie camera, 1900, was cheap and made photography available to the masses. Every man, woman and child had a photograph album. 6. L. Bouton, the father of underwater photography, taking a photograph under water using magnesium light. The camera is on the right. 7. Leitz camera, 1925. The first reliable small hand-held camera was made possible by the invention of faster film, making exposures shorter so the final picture was not blurred. 8. A modern single lens reflex (SLR) camera with an interchangeable telephoto lens.

5   6

7   8

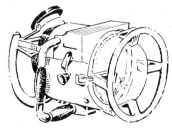

►Hasselblad 500 CM camera in an underwater housing. The Hasselblad is the most commonly used professional large negative camera.

Film-making

▲ English triunial magic lantern, 1890 (right), could show seven pieces of action in rapid time. Filoscope, 1901. Photographs on strips of card, which when flicked created the impression of movement as did the magic lantern.

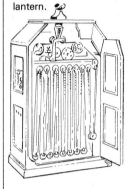

▲ Edison's Kinetoscope (left) contained 15 m of perforated film which could be run at 46 frames per second. This projected a 'movie' of 15 seconds for one person to view. Coin-operated Kinetoscope parlours were all the rage in 1892. Film showing was revolutionized by the first movie projector (right) invented by the Lumière brothers in 1895.

▲ A hand cranked Pathé movie camera (left), 1920. A modern movie camera (right) with its sophisticated sound and lens systems.

▲ A video camera, 1984. Now everyone can produce films that do not require processing. All that is required is the camera, a TV and a videotape recorder.

Indulgences

The gradual development of world-wide trade—especially the discovery of America and the sea-routes connecting Europe with the East—greatly increased human enjoyment by introducing new products, especially foods and drinks, into continents where they had never before been known.

Thus America provided potatoes, artichokes, turkeys, maize and chocolate. Africa provided coffee, bananas, beans and sugar (these were taken to the Americas which eventually became the main exporters). The cocoa bean arrived from Central America and by 1657 'drinking chocolate' was advertised in London, but it was not until 1819 that 'eating' chocolate began to be manufactured commercially by the Swiss. The homely drink, cocoa, was first produced by Van Houten's of Amsterdam as late as 1828.

These and other beverages had a great effect upon social habits. Tea first reached the West from China in 1609. Coffee had been drunk by the Arabs from about 1000, but it was still considered a curiosity when it appeared in Oxford in 1640. Within a generation coffee houses were springing up in all the main towns of Europe and every fashionable hostess had to offer it at home. By 1724 Dominic François Valentyn was complaining that coffee had become so common in Paris that 'unless the maids and seamstresses have their coffee every morning, the thread will not go through the eye of the needle.'

▼ Today very strange animals are kept as pets — panthers, piranhas, caymans, iguanas. This is a pet reticulated python. It is kept in a tank.

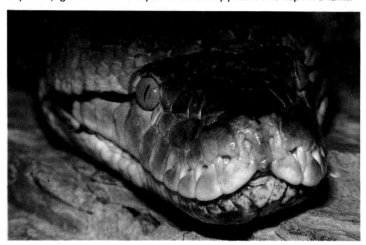

Smoking

▲ King Sethes I of Egypt, burning incense before the god Osiris and Horus, 1300 BC.

▲ Mayan priest smoking, AD 300 (left). West Indian with a forked pipe-stem which he has just used to inhale smoke from a burning tobacco leaf, 1526.

▲ Indian tomahawk pipe (left) could be used for both purposes and was not a pipe of peace. Japanese labourer smoking (right).

▲ *Geisha* girl smoking (left). In 1596, the emperor planted Japan's first tobacco seeds brought by the Portuguese. Chinese water pipe (right).

▲ Indian Nargileh water pipe (left). Water in the bowl removes impurities and cools the smoke. Chinese snuff bottle (right).

▲ South American Indian inhaling tobacco smoke. Ironically they believed tobacco smoke cured disease.

▲ Aristocratic smoking-party in Germany, 1720. Tobacco clubs for men and women sprang up all over Europe.

▲ Madame Vigée-Lebrun smoking (left). Women smoked pipes quite frequently. This one lived to be 87. Indian hookah (right).

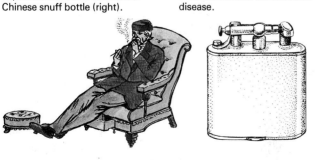

▲ In the late 1890s, a Victorian father could shut himself away wearing his smoking jacket and cap while sitting in his smoking chair. Adoring women folk also embroidered tobacco slippers not for wearing but for hanging on the wall to store tobacco. The first Dunhill lighter, 1910 (right).

◄ King George V and Tsar Nicholas II smoking cigarettes did much to make smoking popular in the 20th century. But the death of George VI, a heavy smoker, from lung cancer, brought home the health hazard of cigarettes until today's cigarette packets actually carry a warning (above).

Not all these new introductions were an unmixed blessing. From America came tobacco, long cultivated by the Indians who found that by smoking or chewing it they experienced a mild form of intoxication and felt less tired. The Spaniards rolled the leaves into cigars, so called from their likeness to the *cigaron*, an Andalusian cricket, and Jean Nicot, introducing the smoking habit to France, gave us the word 'nicotine'. This form of indulgence quickly caught on, was fiercely denounced by King James I and others, but only in modern times has been shown as the cause of countless deaths.

Even sugar—suddenly made cheap and plentiful when the sugarcane plantations were established in the West Indies—is now regarded with less favour. Previously the only sweetener available had been honey which though easy to make had never been mass-produced and consequently was relatively rare. Sugar transformed diets, in particular it made coffee, tea and chocolate popular and, at first, like some of the other new food supplies, it helped in the vast improvement in nourishment of the growing European populations. Only today is it being recognized as an excessive element in diet, not only bad for teeth but contributing to more serious conditions.

Another form of indulgence—alcohol—was known in Europe from earliest times, though the word itself is Arabic and beer may have been brewed first in Mesopotamia. Wine was the regular drink of the Greeks and Romans, but the making of spirits—stronger liquors distilled from wine—came in the 11th century when a Catalan physician used the process for the treatment of wounds and found that by adding aromatic herbs he could produce an agreeable and powerful drink. The Germans called it *Brant Win* (burnt wine) which became brandy in English. It was soon found that wine was not needed for distilling, and that countries without vineyards could produce whisky, gin or vodka from grain, or rum from the molasses of the sugar plantations. Cheap gin was especially the curse of the 18th century, spreading poverty and disease among the working class at home, and (as 'fire water') bringing degradation and disaster to unsuspecting peoples in Africa and America.

▼ The Gin Palace. During the 18th century in Britain, gin drinking became a social evil. The warmth and light of the gin palaces encouraged the ill-housed to flock there.

Pets

▲ Dogs are descended from wolves. They first became tame when wolf cubs were brought back to camp by hunters.

▲ Men in Çatal Hüyük, Anatolia, 6000 BC, kept leopards as sacred pets.

▲ In Anatolia, pet dogs accompanied their dead masters into the grave, so that they could be together in the after-life.

▲ Egyptian queens used to keep pet baboons.

▲ An unkind girl plays with her pet tortoise (left). Roman emperor Caligula used to have a lion that took part in banquets (right).

▲ Chinese fishermen use cormorants to catch fish. They are on a lead and wear a neck ring so they cannot swallow the catch.

The Aztecs kept parrots (left) as pets. They also made good guards, warning off intruders. In 16th-century Italy (middle), bored women tried to keep themselves amused by tending exotic pets. Europeans take dogs for walks. The Muslims of the 16th century had monkeys (right).

▲ A little girl takes her pet dog for a run, 1700.

▲ Falconry was also a popular sport in the 16th century. Falcons killed birds, shrews and even hares.

▲ Mongooses are still kept as pets in India. They kill snakes and seem to be immune to their venom.

Home, Sweet Home

Looking at Houses

From Tents

Ask a little child to draw a house. And most likely it will draw you an oblong, with a door in the middle and windows each side. Yet how many houses *do* have the door in the middle? If the child looked at its own house, it would probably find that it did not.

Houses vary enormously. When we travel abroad we immediately notice that French houses look different from British, and German or Spanish different again. Even within one country houses change from region to region.

People used to build from whatever materials were available— stone from their own hills, timber if they lived near a forest, then brick if they had clay and could make their own. When canals and railways and finally motorways made long-distance transport easy, builders were tempted to use the cheapest materials, wherever they came from. Houses lost their distinctive local look.

Men began to build houses about 10,000 years ago. At first they imitated their former caves—they dug a circular hole and roofed it with reeds, branches, palm-leaves or slabs of turf. About 7000 BC, the first oblong dwellings appeared—a great improvement, since several oblongs could be joined to make a bigger house with separate rooms.

Gradually men learnt to shape stones, bake bricks, mix plaster and cement, and cut timber into beams and planks. In the dry countries, where civilization began, a flat roof was— and is—quite satisfactory. In the northern forest lands, trees were the basic material. Men began by tilting two straight tree-trunks together and lashing them at the end like a V upside-down. Two such pairs were joined by a horizontal ridge-pole, and more logs were added to produce a tent-shaped house that was practically all roof. This was ideal for throwing off heavy rain and snow. This steeply pitched roof remains usual in northern countries to this day.

The upright walls were at first very low, but as centuries passed they were built higher. The roof jutted out above them, as eaves, so that the rain ran off without touching the walls. Then gutters were added to catch the water, and drainpipes to carry it away. The pipes on our modern houses are painted cast-iron or plastic. Quite separate is the wastepipe running down from the lavatory. In Britain the law says it must be outside the house, but in some countries, where the winters are very cold, it has to be fitted inside the building to prevent it bursting. The garden also depends on the climate. Gardening is hardly possible in countries where the soil is frozen deep throughout the winter, and in the hot dry countries plants die if they are not frequently watered.

Today in building a house, factors other than size, shape and decoration have to be considered. The huge cost of energy —electricity, coal and gas, has made people look for ways to conserve it. Most houses are now built with lagged lofts, tightly fitting windows and doors, and double glazing. Some people have gone even further and attempted to use 'free' sources of energy to heat their homes. Solar panels in the roof use the sun to warm the house. Wind can be used to run a generator. Even burning domestic waste in a boiler produces an effective amount of heat.

▲ Russian mammoth-bone hut, 25,000 years ago. Where timber was scarce, hunters made their huts from mammoth bones.

▲ Celtic lakeside dwelling, 1st century AD. Their houses were built on lakes for defence and as a means of using space.

▲ Marshmen of Southern Iraq have been building huts made from reeds for centuries. The row of reed hoops is covered in straw matting.

▲ Mongolian *yurts* are built using a lightweight wooden framework, covered with thick felt. They can easily be taken to pieces and re-built elsewhere.

▲ Indian wigwam. In North America hunters built their wigwams from birch poles covered with birch bark.

▲ Timber framed long houses were built for animals and their owners, 1300. Animals lived at one end, people at the other.

▲ Hebridean black houses have been built for 2000 years. The walls are 2 m thick and the thatch is held down with weighted ropes.

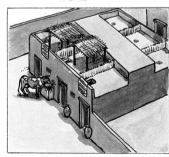

► Egyptian house made from mud brick and plastered. People use the roofs as a recreation area.

To Villas

To Apartments

▲ Greek country house made from soft unbaked mud bricks. The upper floor was held up by wooden beams.

▲ Italian *domus*. The main rooms have an under-floor heating system. Notice the raised pavement for pedestrians.

►Positano, Italy. Houses were originally built up the hill by the fishermen so that they could be near the harbour.

▼A 19th-century English weather-boarded house. Weather-boarding was added to protect the soft timber frame made from newly-imported soft woods when oak became scarce after the 18th century.

▲ Chinese peasant's homestead. The roofs of the living areas are made of tiles. The watchtowers are constantly manned to watch for robbers.

►16th-century English town house. This timber work has been carved to look like the stern of a galleon.

▼A Norwegian house made from spruce timber, 1500, the roof covered with turf as insulation and water-proofing.

▼Pair of semi-detached houses, 1935.

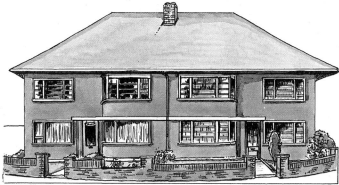

►Dutch terrace, Amsterdam 1662–1665.

▲Casa Milà, Barcelona, designed by Antonio Gaudi, 1905. The most beautiful apartment block in the world.

►Goldberg's Marina City in Chicago USA. Cars are parked at the bottom, offices are in the middle and flats on the top.

Walking In

Doors were always as strong as the householder could possibly make them, given the materials available to him. He could not always have anything as massive as a castle gate, with a portcullis, grille and drawbridge for extra protection, but where possible he had some good solid timber, reinforced with strips and studs of iron. This was also the case in the Near and Far East. Unfortunately, there, more often than not the walls were built of mud bricks, so housebreakers used to break in through the walls. In fact, in Greece, the word for burglar was *toichorychoi*—wall digger.

Our modern front doors are not usually so strong. This is not because we do not fear criminals but rather that they have become more subtle and prefer not to bring a battering-ram when they can find easier ways to get in. The householder, in turn, uses his commonsense and the advice of police and insurance companies to make it harder.

So much for the protection side, today. It must not be forgotten, but we do not spend all our time worrying about it and thinking of our home as a fortress.

In towns the front door used to open straight on to the street—and quite often it still does. There is nearly always a doorstep, even when (in some cases) you step down again to the floor inside. Doorsteps are found in the ruins of ancient cities—they were needed to keep the water out of the house

▲ Hever Castle in Kent, showing the wooden gates, portcullis and drawbridge. The word 'portcullis' comes from the French *porte coulisse* or sliding door.

▲ Bronze relief of Solomon and the Queen of Sheba cast by Lorenzo Ghiberti (1378–1455). The most famous doors in the world are the so-called 'Doors of Paradise' at the baptistery in Florence. The first set of doors were designed by Andrea Pisano in 1331 and were generally considered to be very beautiful. In 1401 the Calimale guild of Florentine merchants decided that they wanted the rest of the doors to be their equal, so a competition was held, which was won by Ghiberti. He designed the doors so beautifully that he was given a free hand to execute the final set. This was his masterpiece. A passer-by saw Michelangelo staring at them in awe and asked what he thought of them. The old man said simply, 'They are fit to be the Doors of Paradise.'

when heavy rain sent it swirling down the street.

Sometimes there is a whole flight of steps up to the door. This may be due to the lie of the land, but often it is to make the house look grander. Noblemen had great staircases of stone sweeping up to their doorways, so why should not lesser folk have at least three or four stone steps if they wanted to appear richer than they were?

Many houses of the 18th century—tall houses now probably turned into flats or offices—have steps like a bridge crossing a railed-off drop between the building and the pavement. This was to allow for cellars and a basement kitchen for the servants, and had its own window, staff door, and steps down to it—the 'ground' floor of the house, perversely, was several feet above the ground.

A house of this period would have a splendid front door, set in a frame with classical decorations. It would have glass panes above it, called a 'fanlight' because they often formed a semicircle like a fan, to let daylight into the hall within. In earlier centuries there was no porch to offer shelter—the overhanging eaves originally did that—but in time a projecting canopy of stone or lead was provided, often very decorative. Then came more elaborate colonnaded porticoes.

Doorknockers are very ancient. Brasenose College at Oxford takes its name from its original bronze knocker, a lion's head, and we know that the scholars removed it when they walked out on strike in 1334. Many people still have doorknockers because they are often beautiful or amusing, but bells are more common, with electricity in place of the bygone wires. Sometimes a knocker is combined with the hinged flap that we still refer to as 'the letterbox', though it is really only a slit in the door and few people fit a box inside to catch the letters. This opening became necessary when the 'Penny Post' (1840) vastly increased the volume of mail.

The postman's work was much helped if the house had a number. That idea began in Paris, just on the Pont Notre Dame, in 1463, but it was slow to spread. When it appeared in London in 1708 it was in a Whitechapel street occupied by refugees from the Continent, and it was not made compulsory in the city until 1765.

Doors

▲ Doorless entrance to Egyptian house, 1900 BC. In very hot countries doors were often dispensed with.

▲ Courtyard of a modern African dwelling. Sticks and animal skins are used to cover the door.

▲ Dutch door (left) opened half way up to let in light and keep out animals. Notice the spy hole. Above the wooden doors (right) hangs a horseshoe. This brings a household luck provided it is hung the right way up. If not the luck drops out of the shoe!

▲ As communities grew, larger doorways (left) were needed to allow animals and carts to enter. Wooden doors were used but these were very heavy to open and to avoid opening and shutting them each time a pedestrian came through a smaller door was built into the main door for their use. In hotter countries doors are open at the top (right). To prevent insects entering, a mosquito net is fitted to the outside.

▲ 19th century Dutch door with a mechanical door-bell.

▲ Two beautiful doors in a Georgian terrace. The windows above the doors are called fanlights, because they are shaped like a fan.

▲ Modern doors vary enormously. This door to a bar in America is in the shape of a keyhole.

▲ Revolving doors are often used in hotels to control the flow of people entering.

Locks & Keys

► First method of keeping things secure was to put them in a hole and cover them with a stone.

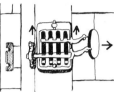

▲ Greek lock (left). The key was inserted into the holes, the catch lifted and the wooden bolt pulled back with the attached rope. Sumerian lock (right) works on the same principle.

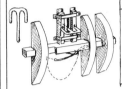
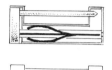

► Chinese padlock in closed position (top). When the 'H'-shaped key (bottom) was inserted it closed the flanges (middle) allowing the lock (shaded) to be pulled out.

▲ Russian padlock, 16th c. (left). Dutch lock, 17th c. (right). The man covers the lock with one of his legs. The leg is extended revealing the keyhole by pushing a secret button. The toe-cap points to a number on a dial which shows the number of times the door has been unlocked. The lock bolt can be released by pushing back his hat.

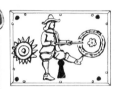
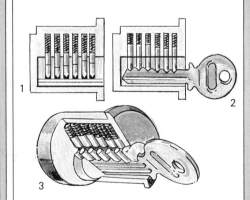

▲ Modern cylinder lock invented by Linus Yale in 1848. 1. Two-sectioned pins of different lengths are pushed down by springs into holes in the cylinder block locking it. The key with the serrations on its edge in the correct sequence pushes each pin upwards so they are aligned and the tumbler can spin free. 2. The key can then be turned to unlock the catch 3.

Lighting

The word window comes from 'wind-hole' which is what the first windows were—an opening in the wall or roof to let in air for the fire. Since, in the winter, the air was extremely chilly most houses had small wind-holes and as few as possible. Some small houses had none at all. The main light source would have been the open door, hence the expression 'never darken my door again'.

To keep out birds and animals the wind-hole often had a light screen of reeds arranged in a cross-cross pattern—a pattern that was echoed in the lead lights of Tudor windows.

The first major changes in the window came with the invention of glass. The Romans had invented glass windows before Pompeii was destroyed in AD 79. Sheets of glass as large as 53 cm by 46 cm and up to 13 mm thick have been found. But glass was far from universal and after the fall of the Roman Empire glass-making went into decline. So we find that most early glass was used in small pieces joined together by narrow lead frames or *cames*. This was expensive and because of their cost windows tended to be small. Their owners treated them

▲ The 'Rose of France' in the North transept of Chartres Cathedral, 13th century.

Windows

▲ Open Norman window. For security and warmth 'windows' were small. Peasants' cottages had no windows.

▲ Sumerian window grille, 3000 BC—used to reduce draughts without cutting off the light completely.

▲ English window, 14th c. Only the top half is glassed because of the expense. In cold weather the bottom half is shuttered.

▲ Bay window, 1530. They first became popular in the 14th c. and have remained so ever since.

▲ Leaded windows, 16th c. Large panes of glass were hard to make. Here little panes are held together in a beautiful pattern by lead *cames*.

▲ Italian window of the High Renaissance. The pediment above the window harks back to the classical architecture of ancient Greece and Rome.

▲ Hinged leaded window, mid 17th c. The wooden frame has to be robust because of the window's weight. This often warped causing the glass to bulge.

▲ Sash window, 18th c. The top half is fixed: only the bottom half can be opened by sliding upwards.

▲ Sliding sash window, 1810. They were easier to fit in the squat openings of low-ceilinged buildings.

▲ French windows are windows that open outwards on to a balcony or garden.

▲ Dormer windows give the extra space to build a room into the roof.

▲ In recent years double glazing has increasingly been used to insulate houses, keeping heat in to save money on fuel bills and keeping noise out.

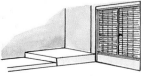

▲ Picture windows came in after WW II. They are made from thick plate glass and allow you to see and be seen.

▲ Traditional Japanese windows are made from oiled paper.

as furniture and removed them when moving house until a law was passed in England banning this in 1579. Windows were hung on hooks to make them easy to remove and so that burglars did not steal these valuable items they were often placed high up on a wall.

To some extent the size and position of a window was also dependent on climate. In hot countries windows were very small set in thick walls. In fact it is out of consideration for climate that stained glass was first used. Mediterranean churches of the 12th century used stained glass to decorate its churches but also to exclude the hot sun. Craftsmen discovered that by adding specific minerals such as copper, iron, silver or gold and carefully controlling conditions in the kiln they could produce glass of different colours.

By 1600 the glass industry was sufficiently established all over Europe for the ordinary family to be able to afford glass in their windows—although some parts did not have glass until the early 19th century. Until then various methods had been used as substitutes—oiled fabric or paper (like the Japanese) or cattle placenta (the Irish preferred a mare's placenta as it was said to be bayonet-proof).

In the late 17th century a change was introduced from Holland that enabled windows to be much larger than before —the sliding sash window made in wood. At first most sash windows were fixed at the top with only the lower part able to move but by the end of the 18th century the counterbalanced double sash had replaced this system.

In recent times aluminium sliding windows have been introduced and large windows with single panes of thick plate glass. Plate glass is now so strong that whole buildings can be made of it removing the need for any windows at all—the United Nations Building in New York and the Vickers Building in London are but two examples of this.

▲ The window tax of 1784 was an ingenious method of taxing the rich. The logic was that if you were rich, you had a large house and therefore more windows than if you were poor. The rich saved money by blocking out windows. This reduced light and fresh air and as a result there was a significant increase in illness, particularly during epidemics.

Lamps

▲ Stone Age lamp. Hollowed out sandstone filled with animal fat and moss for a wick was the main source of night light for centuries.

▲ Lamps found at Ur made from shells and decorated, 3000 BC.

►Chinese lamp, AD 125 (top). These portable lamps were used by all but the poorest families. 14th c. floor candlestick (right). Rich families used tallow candles made from mutton grease. Poor families, unless they were sheep rearers, had to make do with rushes lightly coated with grease. A 60 cm rush gave a good light for half an hour.

▼ Floor standard for rush and candle. The rush had to be burned at an angle so that the falling grease did not extinguish the flame.

▲ Top: Flemish brass chandelier, 15th c. Belgium became a centre for brass chandelier manufacture in the 15th century. Left: Candle mould, 18th c. Right: Italian brass hanging lamp of the 16th c.

▲ Chinese paper lantern (left). The discovery of gas in the early 19th century as a fuel led to its use as a source of light (middle). The Victorian paraffin lamp with a twin-wick duplex burner (right) gave a very bright flame. But for the accidents caused by dropping lamps, it would have presented a serious threat to the popularity of gas lamps.

▲ Brass bedroom candlesticks, 1830, were still used to light the way to bed (left). The breakthrough in lighting came with Thomas Edison's invention of the electric vacuum lamp (middle) in October 1879. Modern lamp, 1983 (right).

Upstairs and Downstairs

Nowadays, when we enter an ordinary house, one of the first things we see is a staircase leading up from a small entrance-hall. Unless, that is, the house is all on ground-level—a 'bungalow'. The word means 'from Bengal' and Europeans who had worked in the East have introduced it within the last century when they retired.

Our forefathers, until about 1500, seldom had stairs to avoid. Houses began as single-room timber halls, with a central hearth and a hole in the roof to let the smoke out. In castles the lord and lady used to dine on a raised platform at the far end of the hall, looking down on all their servants. After a time, wishing to be more private, they built an upstairs room for themselves, going up by a spiral staircase of stone such as we still see in old castles and church-towers.

In the later Middle Ages houses began to have staircases like ours. In the 16th century mansions where the hall was very lofty, they went up in a series of short flights with right-angle turns. One bend at most is usually enough in our modern houses, and we have simple handrails and banisters, whereas prosperous householders in the past used to glory in magnificent and elegant staircases with all sorts of carved

▲ The Great Bed of Ware: Made of oak, it was built in the late 16th century and is 3.25 metres square. In those days the mattress rested not on springs but on ropes. Beds were treasured possessions and were often left as legacies to friends or relations.

wood or wrought iron. Today, when we reach the landing at the top of the stairs, we have separate doors into each bedroom. In the 16th century people had to pass through one room to reach another—which is why people slept in curtained four-poster beds.

Beds

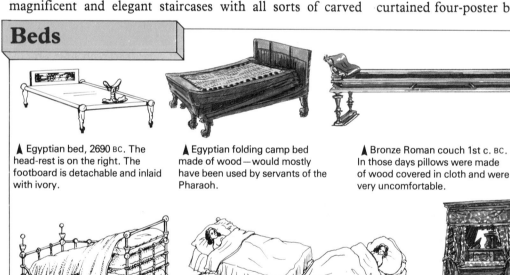

▲ Egyptian bed, 2690 BC. The head-rest is on the right. The footboard is detachable and inlaid with ivory.

▲ Egyptian folding camp bed made of wood—would mostly have been used by servants of the Pharaoh.

▲ Bronze Roman couch 1st c. BC. In those days pillows were made of wood covered in cloth and were very uncomfortable.

▲ 10th c. bed reproduced by Viollet-le-duc (1814–79), the French architect, for sale in the 19th c.

▲ Truckle-bed, 13th c., used by servants—when not in use it was stored beneath a larger bed.

▲ French bed made of walnut with silk brocade, 16th c.

▲ Custom dictated that the Assyrian king dined alone in bed while his wife sat apart. King Sardanapalus committed suicide with his wife and 150 concubines by setting themselves alight in bed.

Chairs

▲ Egyptian chair, 2690 BC (left). Medieval monk's stool (right).

▲ Refectory bench (left), crude bench with a back (right), 13th c.

▲ Chair in the house of a merchant in the 16th c.

▲ Italian folding armchair, 16th c. (left). Chinese Ming hardwood chair, 1500 (right).

Servants in a big house had separate 'backstairs', so that they could do their work without meeting the family as they went up and down with fuel-buckets and slop-pails. But the words 'upstairs' and 'downstairs' were often used in a special way to distinguish the servants from the family—'downstairs' referring to the kitchen and scullery and servants' hall below, while the family and their friends occupied the main rooms overhead. Until the First World War servants were plentiful and cheap. A maidservant could not expect to earn more than 40p a week. A grand house might employ up to 40 servants just working in the houses. Even senior clerks, and similar people, who themselves earned between £3 and £10 each week would employ a maid to do the housework. One woman in three worked as a domestic servant. The Second World War advanced industry and technology and suddenly jobs could be had in the new factories and on production lines. 'Going into service' was now only one of many options open to men and women wanting to earn a wage. This, combined with a shakier economy which greatly raised prices after 1945 put the wages of a servant out of the reach of most people.

The original central hearth and hole in the roof had gone out by the late Middle Ages, to be replaced by stone fireplaces and chimneys—which meant that there could be separate fires in different rooms, even bedrooms. And there often were, so long as there were plenty of cheap servants and fuel.

When wood became scarcer for fuel, with the cutting down of forests after 1500, coal took its place. Its smoke was so

► Marcel Breuer designed this chrome-plated steel tube chair in 1925. It was considered a revolutionary design when it was first shown. It would certainly put the design of some modern chairs to shame. It is now an exhibit in the Museum of Modern Art, New York.

unpleasant that in the 16th century builders began to raise the height of chimneys, adding a tall stack above the roof. Coal, plentiful in Britain, continued as the main source of heat until the mid-20th century, when central heating took over. Central heating was first tried in a French château as long ago as 1777, but the massive pipes and radiators for many years limited it to great mansions and public buildings. The central heating revolution came in the 1950s, when electric pumps enabled the hot water to be circulated through inconspicuous small-bore pipes which could be installed without too much damage to the walls. Solid fuel might still be used to heat the boiler, but first oil, and then gas, began to supersede it, until even in the smaller newly-built houses central heating became the norm.

▲ Bed of Gabrielle d'Estrées, mistress of Henry IV of France. Gabrielle had over 20 beds which she used on a rota basis.

▲ Top: *Chaise Longue* or Day bed, 1680–1700. Above: One of Napoleon's iron camp beds.

▲ Above: American cradle. Below: A Belgian invention providing fresh air without opening a window. Right: Charles Dickens' 'state room' on *S.S. Britannia*, 1842.

▲ Above: Single beds with sociability by Sheraton. Below: Hammock with mosquito net, 1885.

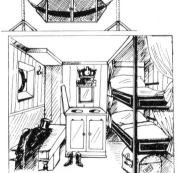

▲ Top: Galvanized steel bed with wire mattress that could support a one tonne weight. Above: American parlour bed, 1891.

▲ Mink covered double bed, 1959, priced at £2,500.

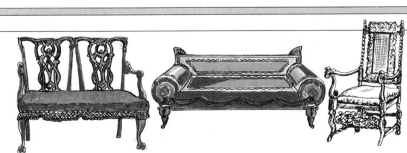

▲ Chippendale settee, 1772 (left). Sheraton sofa, 18th c. (middle). Carved walnut armchair, 1680 (right).

▲ Painted American rocking chair, 1850s (left). Mahogany high chair, 1860 (right).

▲ Mackintosh chair, 1901 (left). Modern chair, 1970s (right).

Cooking Methods

▲ Cooking meat over a fire, 25,000 BC.

▲ Bread being baked in an Egyptian clay oven, 2000 BC.

▲ Roman slave cooking *ligumen*, a sauce made with rotted fish, in an iron saucepan over charcoal.

▲ Two geese and a sucking pig cooking on a spit in front of an open fire. One servant stoked the fire, the other turned the spit.

▲ Cooking in a cauldron. Ginger, cinnamon and saffron were used by the rich to make their food more tasty.

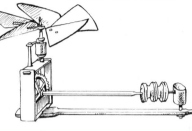

▲ Smoke Jack, 18th c. As the spit rotated, it turned the fan drawing the smoke from the fire up the chimney.

▲ Dog turning a spit, 1790s. If the dog slowed down a hot ember was applied to its heels.

▲ Kitchen at Windsor Palace. Pies were put on the hearth under an iron lid and covered with hot ashes.

▲ Roasting range in a large 19th-century hotel. Four spits could be turned at once.

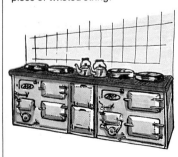

▲ Kitchen, 1850. a clockwork bottle-jack rotates a joint of meat about a vertical axis. It replaced a piece of twisted string!

▲ James Sharp's gas oven, 1850 (left). Gas from jets in the bottom cabinet cooked the food in the middle. The top contained water to keep food hot. Electric hot plates (middle), toaster and steak grill, 1900 (right) from France.

▲ Double Aga cooking range, 1938, suitable for a large house. There are two temperature possibilities.

▲ Electric cooker, 1912. In early cookers, the elements kept burning out and it did not become a rival to gas until 1930.

▲ Microwave oven. The first one was patented in 1953 in the USA. Microwaves cook food much more quickly than normal methods.

Cutlery

▲ Australian aboriginal knife with flint blade. Most people in the age of agriculture carried a knife. Forks did not appear regularly until the 16th century.

▲ Most people ate with their fingers and this type of knife (top). Above: Small forks were used in the 11th c. in Byzantium.

▲ Left: Table forks, 17th c. Right: The knife, fork and spoon used by Louis XIV, king of France (1600s).

▲ Cutlery tended to be made from the materials that were available. These spoons are made from horn and decorated.

▲ Left: Fish knife and fork, 1850. Fish knives were not used for cutting so the blade was blunt and wide to lift the flesh off the bones. Right: Modern Swedish cutlery.

The Kitchen

The kitchen is often the most attractive room in the house—especially when you are young. It is a place of appetizing smells and casual snacks, bustle and company, gossip and heart-to-heart talks. And it is nearly always warm.

Some things in the kitchen have changed very little down the centuries. Basic utensils continue—saucepans and frying-pans for instance—though new materials come in (no aluminium before 1855, when it was first manufactured in Paris) and improvements like the 'non-stick' finish. Good sharp knives are essential, but whereas the cooks of long ago used to whet them on the kitchen doorstep there are now various easier ways of keeping a keen edge. Stainless steel, first made in 1913 in Sheffield, is one blessing that has removed a tiresome chore—the bigger households used to pay a 'knife-boy' to keep the blades bright.

So, though weary mothers may groan that 'cooking always has to go on just the same', it is not exactly the same. The story of kitchens, from Cinderella's time and ages before, is a long interweaving of old traditions and new ideas.

The first cooking must have been over an open camp-fire—or in the hot ashes when it died down. One of the most ancient cooking aids would have been the spit, a thin pointed rod thrust through the meat to hold it in the heat. Cooking *over* the fire meant the loss of fat and juices, so it was better to cook in front of the blaze, with a receptacle (eventually a dripping tin) below the meat to catch the liquid. This meant that the joint had to be turned from time to time, to be cooked all round. In big kitchens—in castles, say—this monotonous job fell to a boy, the 'turnspit'. Then some ingenious unknown had the idea of giving the job to a dog. The dog was placed in a treadmill above the fireside which by a simple gear system kept the spit turning. By the 18th century, mercifully, some one else had devised a clockwork jack to do this work, though the hapless little dogs were still used for a long time.

For poor people their kitchen was the family living room—it had the only fire or stove, and they clustered round it. For the upper and middle classes, though, with servants, the kitchen was a spacious, busy work-place.

Most foods had to be cooked from scratch in days gone by.

▲ Non-stick pans. In 1938, an American chemist, Roy Plunket, discovered by accident a plastic material with remarkable properties—polytetrafluoroethylene. It was unaffected by heat from between −260°C and 330°C, moisture and it was frictionless—nothing stuck to it. These characteristics were exploited in 1958 by Mark Grégoire, a Frenchman, who began manufacturing non-stick frying pans.

The shops (when there were any) sold only basic foods. There were no popular brand names, no labelled packets and cans and bottles, no frozen foods, no 'takeaway' meals, except for hot meat-pies and a few other items that could be bought in the cookshops even in the Middle Ages. Generally speaking, if you wanted bread, jam, cake, biscuits, pickles, and so on, you had to make them. You plucked chickens and skinned rabbits, cured hams and pressed ox-tongue. And except for those items you could preserve yourself, you ate what was in season and—barring one or two things like herring—you ate what was produced locally. There were no special banana ships from the West Indies, no cargoes of New Zealand lamb. Until the 17th century you could not even revive your flagging energies with a cup of tea or coffee.

Things got easier in the 19th century, especially if one was within reach of good shops. Food manufacturers were starting up. They made up food in the factories that had previously only been made at home. If we study some of the labels on our larder shelves we can see how old-established many of the brand names are.

Kitchen Gadgets

The main change in the life of the kitchen began with the decline of the servant. Once the householders had to cook for themselves the design, position and contents of a kitchen dramatically altered. The kitchen was brought out of the basement so that more light was available. Careful design of kitchens made them more compact so that no longer would you have to go on a long walk to get from the sink to the cooker. But by far the greatest kitchen revolution was the invention of new aids—refrigerators, pressure cookers, washing-up machines, potato peelers and mashers, electric mixers, waste disposal sink units and microwave ovens.

These time-saving devices have accompanied big social changes. Many women now have jobs outside the home. Husbands are not only expected to help in the kitchen, but many have discovered a genuine interest in cooking—and developed considerable skill.

There have been reactions too against the changes. Despite the popularity of 'convenience foods' there is a revival in 'home-made' and traditional recipes, and some kitchens are designed in a nostalgic style rather than the ultra modern.

▼ A beautiful example of a compact modern kitchen with all 'mod cons' (modern conveniences).

Heating

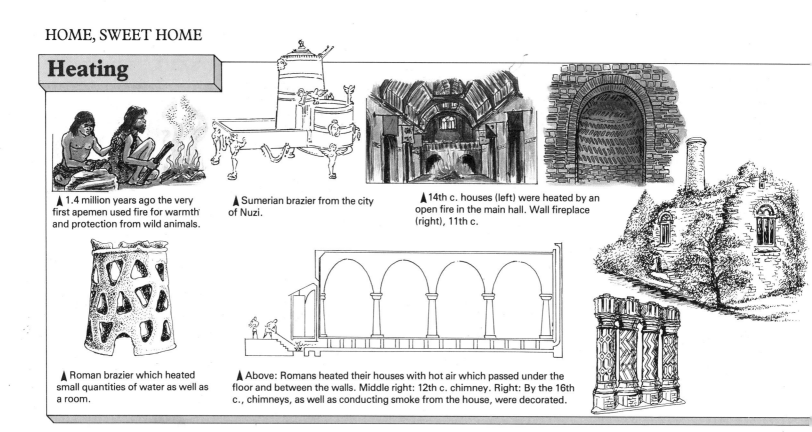

▲ 1.4 million years ago the very first apemen used fire for warmth and protection from wild animals.

▲ Sumerian brazier from the city of Nuzi.

▲ 14th c. houses (left) were heated by an open fire in the main hall. Wall fireplace (right), 11th c.

▲ Roman brazier which heated small quantities of water as well as a room.

▲ Above: Romans heated their houses with hot air which passed under the floor and between the walls. Middle right: 12th c. chimney. Right: By the 16th c., chimneys, as well as conducting smoke from the house, were decorated.

Home Comforts

Prehistoric people had no machines. They had only the strength of their arms and their intelligence to help them gather food, make shelter and fight off marauding animals. But intelligence, allied to nimble fingers, enabled them to construct aids to survival in the harsh prehistoric world.

Most machines exploit the basic principles embodied in what we call 'simple machines'. Although some of these principles seem so simple that even a small child can apply them, to prehistoric people their discovery and application raised their way of life above that of animals. And the 'simple machines' form essential parts of all today's machines which use movement.

Using these simple principles, people invented many amazing machines. In the 3rd century BC, Archimedes, the Greek mathematician who is reputed to have invented the Archimedes screw, is said to have built a system of pulleys with which he could heave a ship ashore entirely by his own efforts. A group of water-powered flour mills built by the Romans near Arles in southern France in about AD 300 must have produced 300 kg of flour an hour.

Nowadays machines help us to make things in factories and to produce food on the land. They help us to dig and to build. In offices they speed up work; in school they help the teachers to teach. And around the home, they lighten the chores. Automatic central heating systems and air conditioning make sure that we live in comfort whatever the weather and burglar alarms guard the buildings when we are away.

The home was probably the last place to feel the impact of the machine age. But in the last 100 years there has been a mechanical revolution there too. The first automatic tea maker, patented by a gunsmith in 1902, displays fascinating ingenuity. The mechanism is started by an alarm clock which

Machines in the Home

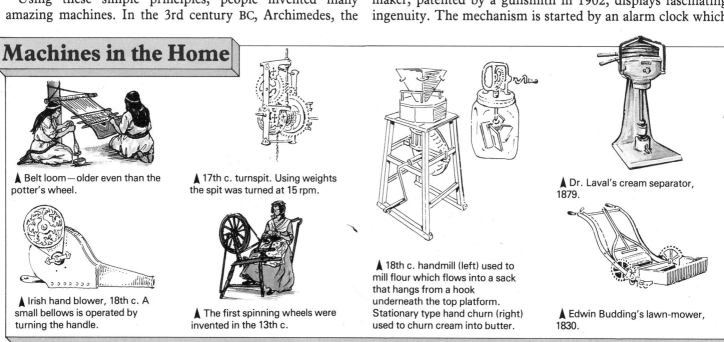

▲ Belt loom—older even than the potter's wheel.

▲ 17th c. turnspit. Using weights the spit was turned at 15 rpm.

▲ Dr. Laval's cream separator, 1879.

▲ Irish hand blower, 18th c. A small bellows is operated by turning the handle.

▲ The first spinning wheels were invented in the 13th c.

▲ 18th c. handmill (left) used to mill flour which flows into a sack that hangs from a hook underneath the top platform. Stationary type hand churn (right) used to churn cream into butter.

▲ Edwin Budding's lawn-mower, 1830.

Americans used cast iron stoves for heating.

1. French water radiator, 1903. 2. Electric glow lamp radiator, 1906.

Top: 15th c. fireplace. It was the custom never to let fires go out. The fire was raked together at bedtime and a cover called a *curfew* (couvre feu) was placed over it. In the morning the curfew would be lifted off and the embers rekindled. Above: 18th c. hob grate.

Portable oil stove, 1890. At first oil was only used for lighting but in 1878 an effective wick for heating was invented.

Gasfire, 1927. After Bunsen solved the early problems of soot in 1855, gas became popular.

Above: Belling electric fire, 1915. Early electric fires were inefficient because the element burned out so quickly. In 1907 a nickel-chromium alloy was developed which marked the beginning of electric fires as we know them today. Below: Fan heater blows the heat from a heated element into the room.

is set to go off at a suitable time. The machine then strikes a match to light a spirit lamp under the kettle. When the water boils, the kettle tips forward and water pours into a teapot placed beside the machine. The spirit lamp is snuffed out and the alarm rings to say that the tea is ready.

More recently, mixers and grinding machines help to prepare the food. We make clothes with sewing and knitting machines. Washing machines wash the clothes and spin dryers dry them. Dishwashers wash and dry the dishes. The rooms are cleaned with a vacuum cleaner or electric polisher. In the bathroom, there are machines for shaving or even cleaning one's teeth. In the garden, we cut the grass and trim the hedges with machines. The do-it-yourself enthusiast extends and maintains the home with a variety of power tools.

All these machines are our slaves, for they cannot function unless we feed energy into them. Yet, in another sense, to many people machines are masters, for once energy has been fed into them they demand attendance.

A solar-heated house in California, USA. For these solar panels to be effective the house needs to be well-insulated. Also solar power is obviously more effective in hot climates than in cold where a costly back-up heating system is needed.

Ewbank carpet sweeper (top). The dust is swept into the box by the sweeper which turns on a cog linked to the wheels. Electric parquet floor polisher (above), 1894.

The hand-operated Baby Daisy used bellows to suck up the dust. The coming of the small electric motor paved the way for advance. In 1901 Hubert Booth devised the filtering method which has been used by cylinder vacuum cleaners ever since.

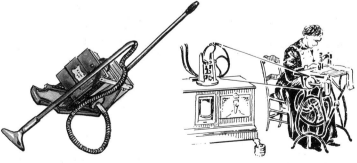

A steam engine being used to drive a sewing machine, 1884.

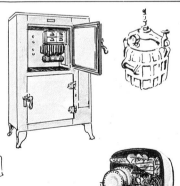

Top left: Domestic refrigerator made by Electrolux in 1927. Top right: Pressure cooker, 1930. Above: Modern dish-washer, first invented in the 1950s.

The Bathroom

Our bathroom may be old-fashioned. It may fall below the standards of luxury and elegance illustrated in the magazines. Yet it has advantages that would have made it the envy of princesses throughout history, even as recently as the 19th century.

Long before the Romans, the people of Knossos, on the island of Crete, had quite good bathroom facilities. Apart from the queen's bath in our picture below, the excavators have found ruins of an inn which had a foot-bath with supply duct, overflow channel and an outlet hole with a stone plug. Another room of this inn has separate bath-tubs of terracotta, and it looks as though they may have had hot running water as well as cold.

It was not until the Romans that the main supplies were really well-organized, with pipes and aqueducts bringing water from great distances. Well-to-do householders could have a private supply run off the public one into their own homes, and they paid according to the diameter of the pipe serving their houses.

Except for the conduits that carried water from rivers to fountains, wells or pumps in different parts of a city, the Middle Ages had no plumbing to speak of. Some lucky people had their own private wells. But most people had to go down to the river, or if they did not live near a river buy water from a water-carrier at the door. However you got your water a lot of hard work or expense was involved, so there was no encouragement to overdo the washing.

▲ A recent addition to the bathroom suite is the *bidet* introduced from France, where it was first used over 200 years ago.

Washing

▲ Egyptian noblemen taking a shower. Bathroom walls were stone waterproofed.

▲ Queen's bath from the Minoan palace of Knossos, 1500 BC.

▲ Mycenaean bath made of stone, 1250 BC.

▲ Greek boy washing off the oil and dirt after playing games in the gymnasium.

▲ 12th c. scullion washing dishes in a sink. Note the drain, which leads to the outside of the castle.

▲ Medieval wall basin (left) and wash stand (right). The rich usually washed in the morning and before meals.

▲ 15th c. wooden bath. Men often used to bath together to conserve water.

▼ 17th c. lady washing. By now soap was widely in use. First made by the Sumerians in 3000 BC, soap was in use by AD 800 in Europe.

Lavatories

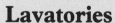
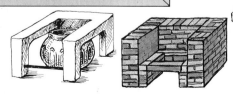
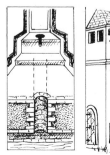

▲ Egyptian 'lavatory' (left). Lavatories in Mohenjo Daro, India in 1900 BC (middle) were made of brick and connected by chutes to the main drains. Limestone lavatory seat from Sumeria (right).

Far left: Roman water closets were connected directly to the sewers. Left: 10th c. latrine built between houses. Above: a *garde-robe* consisted of an opening directly above the moat.

The nobility, of course, could enjoy an occasional tub full of steaming scented water—they had servants to fill and empty it, and pass the towel—but most people, if they took a bath at all, went to a public bath-house. The monasteries were the most concerned with cleanliness—their rules usually stipulated several hot baths a year and in some abbey ruins we can still see the stone troughs in the *lavatorium* where they washed their hands before meals. Monasteries were nearly always built near a river or stream and the stream would be diverted through a pipe to provide running water. Such pipes would be of lead or hollowed elm trunks or of earthenware. Earthenware pipes had first been used in 1500 BC for sewers and latrines in Mesopotamia and in the Indus Valley.

Elizabeth I's godson, Sir John Harington, designed the first water-closet in 1589, but the idea could not be developed for a long time. It needed a main water-supply and it needed also a specially-designed waste-pipe connecting it with a sewer, to prevent dangerous diseases. So people had to continue in the old ways, with earth-closets in the yard or at the end of the garden, and chamber-pots and close-stools under the bed at night. Not until 1778 were the first WCs manufactured in large numbers.

By the 1870s the bathroom was at last evolving as a separate room in the house. Hitherto, people had used hip-baths in their bedrooms. Working-class families until well into the 20th century had their bath in the kitchen, and the bath itself was a common sight hung on the wall outside the backdoor.

Then in 1868 a London decorator, Benjamin Waddy Maughan, invented a gas water-heater which he called a 'geyser'. With this wonderful (but at times alarming) device the luxury of a hot bath was available in minutes.

With so many of these developments so comparatively recent it is surprising that we have had toothbrushes since 1649, dentifrice since 1660, and toothpaste in tubes (instead of pots) since 1891.

► Modern lavatories are made from all sorts of materials—metal, wood, earthenware. This one is plastic with an earthenware bowl. Flushing mechanisms are also very different from earlier models. This lavatory flushes automatically when the lid is closed. The 'Singing Loo' is a model that plays music when sat upon.

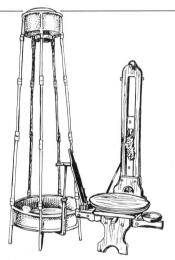

▲ Early shower, 1840s (left). Water from the basin was pumped by hand into the shower head to fall on the bather. Hand shower (right), 1870s. As the lever pumped water on the bather's head, it also moved a back-scrubbing brush.

▲ Twyfords basin with mirror combination, 1899 (top). By the end of the 19th century rooms specially converted as bathrooms with hot and cold water were common. Previously an ordinary room had been used with a fireplace and movable bath (above).

▲ Bath with portable paraffin heater, 1882.

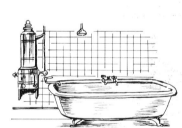

▲ Ewart's patent geyser with shower attachment. A girl could now wallow in a hot bath without mother worrying about the effect of cold water on her complexion.

▲ Shower, 1915. By this time people had begun to look on baths and showers as an 'enjoyable pleasure' and not as necessary items of cleanliness.

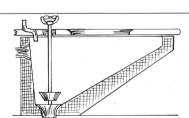

▲ Plug closet of 1750. To flush, you 'pulled the plug' and turned on a tap.

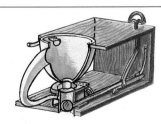

▲ Bramah's closet, 1778. A flap valve was operated by a cranked arm.

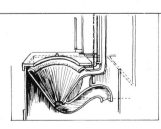

▲ Stephen Green's self-flushing closet, 1849, used a water-filled U-bend as a barrier to the smell.

▲ Doulton's pedestal water closet, 1888, almost identical to the modern cistern lavatory.

Counting and Calculating

When we are quite little playing hide-and-seek, we count up to 100, yell *'Com-ing!'*, and start searching. Gabbling the numbers is the easiest part.

A caveman's children could not have done it. Even their hairy father would not have known the words for all those numbers. He counted on fingers and thumbs up to 10, which is why we have a decimal system now. When he had counted ten wolves it was more than enough. Time to gasp 'Many, many!' and seek safety.

When people began to herd animals they had to count them to make sure not a single sheep or goat was missing. They needed bigger, exact numbers, like 127. And when they became more civilized, building a house of mud bricks, say, they had to measure and use still bigger numbers. 'How many more bricks shall we need?' It was no longer just a question of counting things they could see, they had to calculate the invisible bricks that were not yet made. Our word 'calculate' comes from the Latin *calculus*, a 'pebble', useful for sums

when you get beyond fingers and toes.

The Sumerians led the way in ancient mathematics and astronomy, but, as in other ways, they were rivalled by their neighbours in Egypt. Both countries were using written numerals by about 3000 BC. The Egyptians had a special need for geometry, because their fields were flooded every year by the Nile and the boundaries often had to be marked out again. Geometry was at first worked out by their priests. Later, when the empire of the Pharaohs had declined, the outstanding mathematical progress was made by Greeks living in Egypt where many intellectuals had settled.

It was Euclid, in the Greek-built city of Alexandria in about 300 BC, who created an orderly system of geometry. Eratosthenes, who became chief librarian of that city about 235 BC, calculated the circumference of the earth by comparing the angles of the sun's shadow at different places—and came remarkably close to the right figure.

The earlier Egyptians had had some notion of algebra, but it was another Alexandrian Greek, Diophantus, who pioneered its study in about AD 350. Like other forms of learning it was lost after the fall of the Roman Empire, but it had been developing even earlier in India, and from there it was passed on to the Arabs. We get the word 'algebra' from the title of the first Arab textbook on the subject *Al-jebr* in about AD 820. It

Calculators

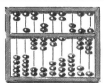

▲ Chinese abacus. The beads above the crossbar represent 5, the ones below—one. The abacus is still used in parts of the world.

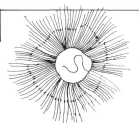

▲ Incas of Peru kept their accounts on *quipus*—cords whose length, colour and knots had different values.

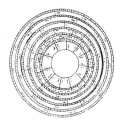

Above: Oughtred's circular slide rule (1622) used the newly-invented logarithms to simplify multiplication and division.

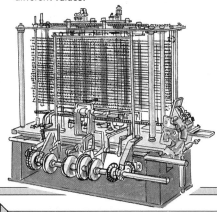

Above left: Rearrangeable multiplication tables devised by John Napier in 1617, one of the forerunners of the slide rule. Above right: Blaise Pascal's calculating machine was the first true mechanical calculator (1642). It could only add but a gearing system allowed numbers to be carried over. Right: Giovanni Poleni's calculating machine of 1709. Left: Charles Babbage invented the first real computer—his Analytical Engine. Babbage never actually built it. The machine was built later from his detailed notes.

POLENI

Numerals

The abacus was used by the ancient Egyptians and later by the Greeks and Romans because their numbers were very difficult to work with. How would you like to add CXLVI and XXXVI? The breakthrough came 1500 years ago when the Indians introduced the zero and a system where the position of a number indicated

▼	▼▼	▼▼▼	▼▼▼▼	▼▼▼▼▼	▼▼▼▼▼▼	▼▼▼▼▼▼▼	▼▼▼▼▼▼▼▼	▼▼▼▼▼▼▼▼▼	◄	Babylonian
Α	Β	Γ	Δ	Ε	Ζ	Η	Θ	Ι	Κ	Greek
Ι	ΙΙ	ΙΙΙ	ΙV	V	VΙ	VΙΙ	VΙΙΙ	ΙX	X	Roman
一	二	三	四	五	六	七	八	九	十	Chinese
•	••	•••	••••	━	⚊•	⚊••	⚊•••	⚊••••	◡	Mayan
٤	٢	٣	٨	५	६	७	८	९	०	Indian

whether it referred to hundreds, tens or units meaning only the symbols 0–9 need be used to write any number. All these concepts reached Europe through the Arabs by 1200 but were not accepted until 1500.

Babylonian: the same symbols were used for writing and counting.

Maya: curved lines multiplied the numbers 20 times.

was not until 1202 that an Italian merchant, Leonardo of Pisa, brought back the forgotten subject to the West.

Mathematics indeed owes a great deal to merchants. Accurate calculations meant profit and loss to them. Merchants had to keep accounts, calculate transport charges and other items, and of course take stock, measure and weigh their goods, and so on. As early as 1489 John Widman's book, *Mercantile Arithmetic,* appeared in Leipzig, giving merchants of the time the useful + and − sign, to save writing *plus* and *minus.* And it was in the great trading city of Bruges that Simon Stevin in 1585 laid down the correct use of the decimal point which had been invented a century before.

The 16th and 17th centuries were a period of tremendous changes in mathematics. They saw the invention of practical aids like logarithm tables invented by John Napier in 1614 and the slide rule by the Rev. William Oughtred in 1621, while on the theoretical side there were pioneer geniuses such as Isaac Newton (1642–1727). In our own day we have seen an amazing technical revolution with the invention of the computer, which can perform our most complicated calculations in the blink of an eye. From a simple bank-statement to the complex planning of a satellite-launching, the electronic computer (started as a war-time device only in 1943) has become an indispensable feature of modern living.

▼ ENIAC (Electronic Numerical Integrator and Calculator) completed in 1946, was the first really electronic machine. It had 18,000 valves that kept burning out at an alarming rate. In fact, ENIAC was not a real computer but a calculator since it did not have a memory. But it did work more than 1000 times as fast as the most up-to-date electro-mechanical machines of that time. A year later came EDVAC (Electronic Discrete Variable Automatic Computer). This was a true computer. It had a memory in which both instructions and data could be stored. And it could change its own programs.

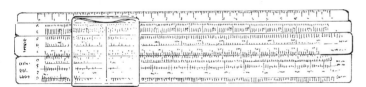

▲ A modern slide rule will allow you to square and cube numbers, inverse ratios, multiply and divide, calculate metric conversions, sine, tangent and cosine angles.

▲ Electronic calculator. Since their invention in 1971 they have reduced in size and in price from about £70 to under £5.

◄ Left: Hollerith invented the first electric calculator. The counting was done by clocks which moved on each time a circuit was completed. It was first used in 1890. Hollerith's business later became IBM. Below: Modern manual calculator, 1950.

▼ Cash register 1879. The first model resembled a clock, one hand indicated dollars and the other cents.

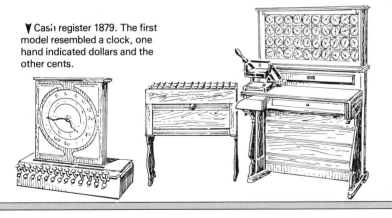

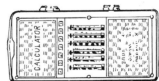

▲ Modern microcomputer. The invention of the microprocessor — basically an entire computer on a single silicon chip — revolutionized the computer industry. Today the simplest computers are the size of a book and cost under £100.

١	٢	٣	٤	٥	٦	٧	٨	٩	٠	Arabic
										Spanish AD 976
										W. Europe AD 1360
										Italy AD 1400
1	2	3	4	5	6	7	8	9	10	0	Modern Arabic
										Computer

Arabic: zero was originally indicated by a dot.

Right: 1 to 10 in binary. Binary numbers seem rather awkward to us—almost like going back to unwieldy Roman numerals. But the binary system is the only one computers recognize, and because the computer operates at such a fantastic speed it can churn its way through millions of 0s or 1s before we can add 2 and 2.

1
10
11
100
110
111
1000
1001
1010

Measuring

▲ In early times parts of the body were used for measuring. A cubit was the distance from a man's elbow to the tip of his finger.

▲ The Egyptians developed the equal arm balance to weigh grain about 7000 years ago.

►Top: Cubit rule. Middle and bottom: Curved calipers and a pair of dividers. The word caliper is a corruption of the word 'calibre' meaning size of something. Calipers usually consist of two equal arms hinged at one end and both have been used since antiquity. The curved calipers would be used with a foot rule, the straight calipers have a scale attached to one arm and were used in navigation to measure distance on a map.

▲ A Roman *groma*, used for laying out right angles. The surveyor looks along the metal rule and lines up the man holding the piece of string. He then repeats the process along the other rule.

▲ The ship's log measured the speed of sailing ships. It was attached to a line and thrown astern, the line being run out for a fixed period. Then the line was hauled in and the length measured. Later refinements were made to give greater accuracy—a half minute sandglass, and knots were tied at intervals of 7 fathoms or 42 feet (12.8 m). The number of knots going outboard during the timed period was then assumed to be the speed of the ship in nautical miles or knots per hour.

►Galileo's thermoscope (left). As the air in the bulb became warmer it expanded, driving the column of liquid down. In 1592 a scale was added so that it was possible to measure this rise and fall. Torricelli's barometer, 1644 (right). He filled a tube, sealed at one end, with mercury and immersed the open end in a bowl of mercury. The mercury fell in the tube but only a little way. Torricelli concluded that the pressure of the atmosphere pushed mercury from the bowl up the tube. He also observed that the height of the column changed and when the level was low the weather was stormy. By 1649, barometric readings were being used in weather forecasts.

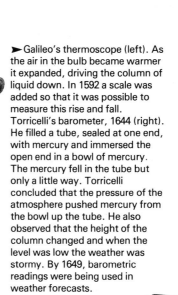

▲ Protractor for measuring angles. Right: Electricity meter to measure electricity used.

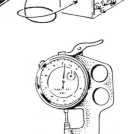

◄ Top: Geiger counter measures radioactive alpha and beta particles. Hans Geiger, while working with the New Zealand physicist, Ernest Rutherford, in 1908, devised an apparatus to count these invisible particles. Geiger counters have become an essential tool in prospecting for radioactive elements. Bottom: This micrometer measures paper thickness. The paper is placed between two studs underneath the dial. The distance that the studs are pushed apart shows on the dial. It can measure something as thin as 1/100th mm.

▲ Wynne's Infallible Actinometer, 1895, enabled photographers to measure the amount of light available. A piece of printing paper darkened when exposed to light. The time taken to darken to match a standard tint was measured and with the aid of tables the exposure details were worked out.

Clocks

▲ Egyptian water clock (left). Water dripped from a hole in the base. Egyptian shadow clock (middle). Chinese water clock (right). Every 24 seconds a scoop becomes full and its weight presses down a trip lever moving the clock round one notch.

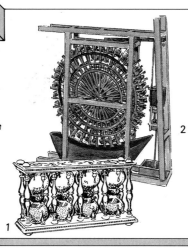

1. Set of sandglasses, 1720, measured the ¼, ½, ¾ and one hour (hence your time is running out). 2. Hour candle. 3. Portable sundial. 4. De'Dondi's clock measured time, days, zodiac signs, motions of sun, moon, planets and feast days.

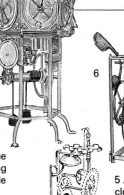

5 .Monastic alarm clock, 15th c. 6. Salisbury cathedral clock mechanism, 1386.

The Nature of Things

The ancient Greek civilization was rich. It had money from its conquered states, from silver mines and from trade. The difference between Greece and earlier civilizations was that the wealth was distributed more democratically, so most people had some money and not every minute of the day was spent trying to survive—a tiring pursuit that leaves no time to be inquisitive. The Greeks were inquisitive people and loved discussion.

Socrates (died 399 BC) was the world's greatest discussion-group leader. He made his friends think by asking apparently innocent questions. He and his young follower, Plato, were chiefly interested in ideas and conduct. But when Plato later founded an informal sort of college, the Academy, he had a brilliant student, Aristotle, who was equally fascinated by the solid world before his eyes. Plato called him 'the reader' and 'the mind of the school'. Aristotle became for a time tutor to the future Alexander the Great. But his own lasting achievement was to start the system of 'scientific classification', observing animals and dividing them up into their different orders and species. What he did for animals his follower, Theophrastus, did for plants, founding the science of botany.

Aristotle was not always right. An earlier Greek, Democritus, was correct when he taught that the whole world was made up of atoms, but his theory was not believed. Aristotle, on the other hand, said that all matter was made up of the four elements, earth, air, fire and water, and this was accepted as truth for many centuries afterwards.

As happened with other forms of knowledge, when the Roman Empire fell, Greek science was preserved for Europe by the Arabs and returned in the Middle Ages. But in many fields the Arabs made considerable progress themselves, especially in chemistry. Their own Jabin ibn Hayan, in the 9th century AD, used chemical apparatus which the West did not improve upon until the 18th century.

Our present attitude to scientific thinking really began early in the 17th century. Francis Bacon (1561–1628) found at Cambridge that the teaching of ideas owed too much to the methods of Aristotle, and he felt a whole new approach was needed, with every theory tested by carefully recorded experiments.

A wonderful age of progress followed over the next century or two. In 1660 the Royal Society was formed, where scientists of every kind could meet, watch demonstrations and exchange ideas. In 1789, a Frenchman, Lavoisier, gave a systematic account of chemical knowledge. Before that, Carl Linnaeus in Sweden (1707–1778) had done the same for botany.

Man's understanding of the earth itself—geology—stems from the great work of Sir Charles Lyell, published in 1830–1833. It greatly influenced Charles Darwin, who in 1831 made a long voyage to the Pacific and South America as a botanist and zoologist aboard *HMS Beagle*. It helped to convince him that the world must be millions of years old, an idea crucial to his treatise on evolution published later and which was to cause such controversy.

The 19th and 20th centuries have seen unceasing scientific research and the advancement of new ideas and discoveries, some transforming the way we live, others altering the way we think. But perhaps four are worthy of special mention. Watson and Crick's work in discovering DNA has led to a deeper understanding of human genetics. In quite another field of study, Sigmund Freud's theories of psychoanalysis have radically altered views on sex, education, crime and human behaviour in general. Ernest Rutherford's splitting the atom opened the door to the era of nuclear power and Albert Einstein's Theory of Relativity elaborated and improved on the ideas of time and space first propounded by Sir Isaac Newton 250 years before.

▲ Mechanism of a caesium atomic clock. The most accurate clock known to man, it would lose one second in 30,000 years.

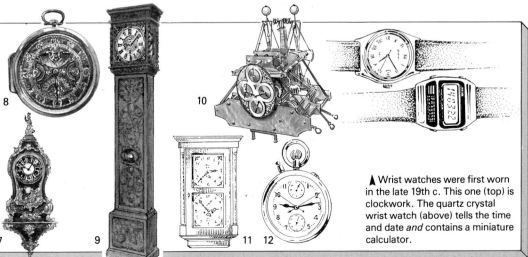

7. Louis XIV French mantel clock. 8. English silver pocket watch. 9. 17th c. English longcase clock by Edward Speakman. 10. Harrison's first marine chronometer, 1735. Kendall's adaptation of it was taken on Captain Cook's second voyage to Australia. 11. Waterwheel clock, 1810. Installed at Park Green Mill. The top clock lagged behind the bottom one when the mill fell behind schedule. The men had to make up the lost time before going home. 12. A stop watch used to time races with two second hands which could be started together but stopped separately.

▲ Wrist watches were first worn in the late 19th c. This one (top) is clockwork. The quartz crystal wrist watch (above) tells the time and date *and* contains a miniature calculator.

Telescopes

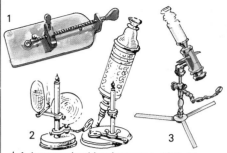

▲ Two of Galileo's telescopes as they are exhibited in the Science Museum in Florence.

▲ An astronomical telescope with two convex lenses and a wider field of view than Galileo's (17th c.)

▲ Newton's reflecting telescope (right). Top: Diagram illustrating the refracting telescope which had the coloured fringe problem. Newton discovered that light of all colours is reflected in the same way by a mirror, so by using a mirror to deflect the light coming into his telescope through the eyepiece (above) he eliminated the coloured fringe around the image.

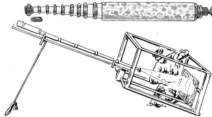

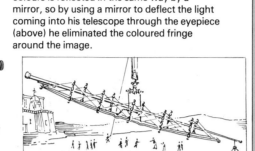

▲ Like most telescopes of the time this English telescope, 1680 (top), is made with draw tubes to shorten it when not in use, hence telescoping. Scheiner's telescope system (above) projected the image on to paper.

▲ During the 18th century ridiculously long refracting telescopes were made. It would have been impossible to see out of the end of this 21-metre Roman telescope.

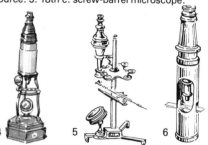

▲ 17th c. theodolite used to measure horizontal and vertical angles in surveying.

▲ Lord Rosse's 6 foot (1.8 m) aperture reflecting telescope. In 1845, it was the largest in the world.

▲ 26 inch refractor telescope, US Naval Observatory.

▲ 200 inch Hale reflector telescope in California.

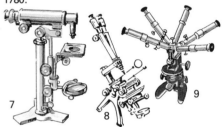

▲ A Schmidt-Cassegrainian telescope has a correcting plate at the point where the light enters the telescope. This gives a sharper picture over a larger area of the sky than other telescopes.

Above: By using two prisms the length of the light path is doubled while keeping the size of the binoculars small enough to be portable. Below: 8 movable dishes of a radio telescope set closely together act as a single dish 5 kilometres across. This one is at Cambridge, England.

Microscopes

▲ 1. Leeuwenhoek's microscope, 1673. The specimen is positioned on a pointed rod and viewed from the other side through a minute lens. The long screw moved the specimen precisely into the line of sight. 2. Robert Hooke's compound microscope and light source. 3. 18th c. screw-barrel microscope.

▲ 4. Culpeper-type microscope, 1740. 5. Microscope 1746. 6. Brass drum microscope, 1780.

▲ 7. Brass microscope, 1880. 8. Binocular microscope, 1890. 9. Late 19th c. microscope with 5 eye-pieces for class work.

▲ Binocular microscope, 1926, with a light condenser unit.

▶The principal advantage of the electron microscope (right) over the ordinary optical microscope is that its power of magnification is much greater—up to 200,000 times is possible. With such magnification scientists are able to study the internal structure of matter.

Mapping the Unknown

In Hereford cathedral there hangs a map of the world, drawn on vellum in about 1300. You can make out Europe, Asia and Africa, though they do not look much like the continents shown in a modern atlas. This world, as men imagined it in those days, is round and flat, with Jerusalem in the centre, and ocean all round the edges. In the blank regions, where the map-maker has really no idea what is there, he has drawn monsters.

It is only 500 years since men began to explore and seek a more complete idea of the earth on which they lived. There *were* earlier explorers. Hanno, a Carthaginian, sailed round Africa in about 500 BC and the Egyptians also knew the route. Then it was forgotten for centuries and had to be found again.

Pytheas, a Greek from Marseilles, at about the time of Alexander the Great, ventured through the Straits of Gibraltar, braved the Bay of Biscay, and coasted up the eastern side of Britain. He was a good navigator and could fix his latitude by astronomical observation.

Much later, just after AD 1000, the Norsemen sailed south from their Greenland settlements as far as Newfoundland. Thus they reached America 500 years before Columbus, but as their discovery led to no developments, and remained unknown to other Europeans, it did nothing to change history. By that date, in fact, Europe had forgotten more geography than it had known in Roman times.

The first known westerner to have visited China and brought back a full account was the Venetian, Marco Polo. In 1295 he arrived home after twenty-four years' absence, having crossed the Gobi Desert, visited Peking, seen India and Indonesia, and sailed back as far as the Persian Gulf. Marco Polo dictated a book on what he had seen. Europe at last knew something about the Far East.

The next man to enlarge our knowledge of the world was a Portuguese prince, Henry the Navigator. He built an observatory and founded a school of navigation, sending out ships to explore the west coast of Africa.

Soon came a tremendous stimulus to such voyages. The rise of Turkish power in the Near East cut off the old overland trade with India and China. Was it possible to continue that valuable business in Asia by sea? Columbus, confident that the world was round, sailed westwards across the Atlantic

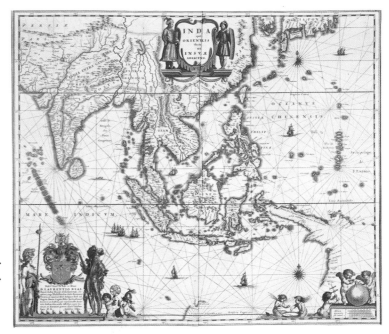

Guillaume Bleau's 1635 map of the Far East, including the East Indies. It is the first map to depict Australia in any form.

intending to reach the eastern shores of Asia. He was unaware of the fact that America blocked his way! So when he reached Cuba in 1492 he believed it was part of India. Five years later Vasco Da Gama set off to get there by another route, round the Cape of Good Hope—and succeeded.

Soon other explorers were rushing to investigate the 'New World'. Amerigo Vespucci reached South America in 1499 and gave such a vivid account that the continent was named after him. Gradually the vast interior was explored and revealed. A Spaniard, Coronado, reached the Rio Grande in 1540. Champlain, a Frenchman, founded Quebec and by making friends with the Indians was able to travel inland between 1603 and 1616.

Gradually this vast blank on the globe was filled in. Magellan was the first to sail the Pacific, and, though he was killed in the Philippine Islands in 1521, in one of the greatest voyages of all time his crew sailed on and were the first to circumnavigate the globe.

Another continent, Australia, remained almost unknown until Captain Cook's arrival in 1770. It had been glimpsed by the Dutchman, Tasman, in 1642 and again in 1699 by the brilliant navigator Dampier—the man, incidentally, who rescued the castaway, Selkirk, on whom the character 'Robinson Crusoe' was based. But it was Cook who literally put Australia on the map, and 19th century explorers like Sturt and Eyre who opened up its desert interior.

Curiously enough it was Africa that was still spoken of as 'the Dark Continent', though much of it had been known in outline from early times. The 19th century saw a rush of exploration to discover its secrets—and a rush of imperial powers to carve up its territory afterwards. A Scotsman, Mungo Park, underwent appalling hardships to explore the River Niger, only to perish in its rapids in 1806. Major Laing crossed the Sahara in 1826.

Today we can say that men have been almost everywhere, including both the Poles. There are however still areas of the world on which man has not set foot . . . parts of northern Alaska, and of the Amazon River basin, the Himalayas, Micronesia, New Guinea and the Arabian desert.

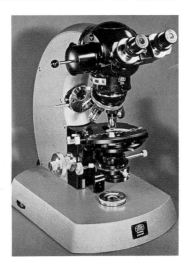

► A Zeiss microscope. This type of microscope is used in research laboratories and has 5 different objective lenses. The highest magnification would be about × 2000.

Physicians and Surgeons

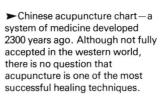

▲ Greek physician.

► Chinese acupuncture chart—a system of medicine developed 2300 years ago. Although not fully accepted in the western world, there is no question that acupuncture is one of the most successful healing techniques.

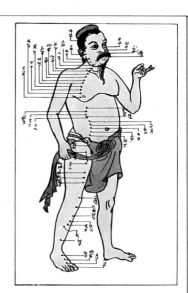

▲ Primitive witch doctor. In primitive societies disease was thought to have been caused by angry spirits. His job was to find out which one and to placate him.

▲ Egyptian physician treating a man with lockjaw. Egyptians were highly-skilled diagnosticians, surgeons and herbalists.

▲ A game of chess is sufficient distraction for the surgeon to operate on this Chinese general for an arrow wound

1. Arab physician AD 900. 2. Outside the towns education was mainly confined to monks in the 11th and 12th centuries. Because of this monasteries became the main source of care for the sick. 3. Doctors during the plague covered themselves completely. 4. Physician, 1562.

▲ Quack doctors preyed on the fears and superstitions of 17th century Europe, offering pills and potions to cure ills.

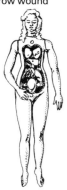

▲ Medicine Elk was a *shaman* (placator of gods) of the Oglala Sioux —a tribe of North American Indians.

► Florence Nightingale revolutionized nursing and became known as the 'Lady with the Lamp' because of her devotion to duty during the Crimean War. She later helped form the Red Cross.

▲ This ivory figure with removable organs was used in the 16th c. for the teaching of midwives!

▲ Herbalists are rare in the west. However in the Third World, the local medicine man does very well making remedies from plants.

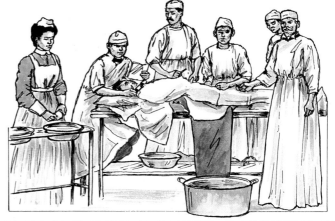

▲ A physician, surgeon and apothecary at a patient's bedside. From 1500 for 300 years there was an intense rivalry between these three branches of medicine.

An American country doctor (above), 19th c. Operating room with the surgeon demonstrating an operation to students, 1902 (right).

Their Tools

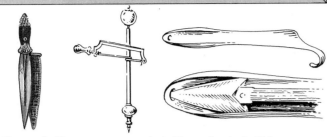

▲ First medical instruments were adapted from other tools. This Sumerian hunting dagger (left) was used for surgery. The Greek bone drill (middle) had been used for kindling fires. The Spoon of Diokles (right) is an early custom-made instrument for extracting arrow heads.

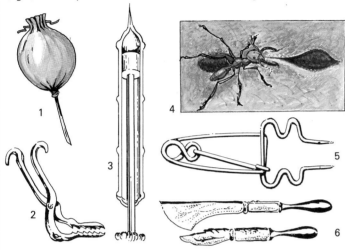

1. Greek syringe—animal bladder tied to a feather shaft. 2. Hindu iron forceps. 3. Greek 'pus-puller' used on wounds. 4. Jaws of dead Eciton ants used as wound clamps. 5. Roman vein clamp. 6. Roman scalpels.

▲ Lancet used for smallpox vaccine, 1800.

▲ Top: Military surgeon's kit, 18th c. Above: 19th c. surgical instruments, including a mechanical saw, forceps and tourniquet.

▲ Ebony 'scarifier', 19th c. The hollow handle was filled with vaccine which was forced out of the 20 fine needles into the arm.

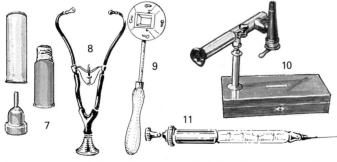

▲ 7. René Laennec's first stethoscope used by a French army surgeon in 1815. 8. Binaural stethoscope 1860 was a modification of 7. 9. Helmholtz's opthalmoscope used for examining the retina of the eye. 10. First opthalmoscope with a light, 1869. 11. 19th c. glass and metal hypodermic syringe. The needle was sharpened for further use.

Medicine

Prehistoric bones dug up show what diseases cavemen suffered and even sometimes the treatment they received. There were even primitive attempts at brain surgery—holes were made in the unfortunate patient's skull to let the evil spirits out—and sometimes the bone has continued to grow revealing that he recovered.

The ancient Egyptians provided free medical treatment through their priests but it was well mixed with magic spells. The Hindus were skilled with drugs and even managed some plastic surgery, especially on noses. And at a very early date the Chinese were using acupuncture, sticking needles into the body at carefully-chosen places, a treatment which they still use—even carry out operations on out patients who are wide awake without their feeling pain. Acupuncture has been recently introduced to the West and gradually its healing power is getting greater acceptance.

In the West, though, doctors trace their profession back to a Greek, Hippocrates, born on the island of Cos in about 460 BC. We call him 'the father of Medicine' and the proper conduct of a modern doctor to his patient is still based on rules laid down in 'the Hippocratic oath'.

Hippocrates did not believe in magic spells. He studied his patients and their symptoms, compared these with what he had observed in earlier cases, and tried to find out what was really the matter, and how best to cure it. Though he did not know a thousand and one things known to the most inexperienced doctor today, Hippocrates had the right scientific approach and passed it on.

The next great name is Galen, a Greek doctor born in AD 130, who moved to Rome in AD 160. He knew more about anatomy than Hippocrates did. It was not easy to learn this science because the dissection of human bodies was against the law. But Galen's first appointment was as doctor to a school of gladiators, and the fearful wounds they received in the arena showed him what lay under the skin. Galen was first to discover how the muscles are controlled by the brain. He wrote 500 books which had an influence—not always good— for more than a thousand years afterwards.

In 1616 William Harvey, later doctor to Charles I, discovered that blood circulated around the body. He was the

▼ Instruments laid out for a spinal operation. Note the special clamps, probes, hammers and chisels that are required. Each area of surgical specialization has developed its own special instruments.

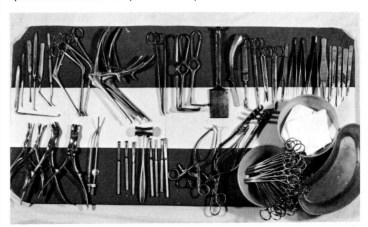

first man to have the idea that the heart acted like a pump, another milestone in medical knowledge. Such knowledge was now steadily increasing, though a great deal of ignorance and superstition was still mixed up in it.

From the 16th century there were three branches of medicine attached to guilds all in intense competition with each other: apothecaries, surgeons and physicians. In 1518 the physicians left their guild to found a College and were granted a licence to practice medicine within seven miles (11 km) of the centre of London.

The apothecaries were still trying to free themselves from the grocers' guild when the physicians tried to stamp them out. Unsuccessfully as it turned out because the apothecaries did not confine their practices to the rich. Adam Smith described the apothecary as 'The physician of the poor in all cases, and of the rich when the distress is not very great', which is a sort of backhanded compliment.

The surgeons were also trying to escape from low company. They had formed a joint company with the barbers in 1540. But as the surgeons became more respectable (and richer) largely through the life-work of one man the surgeon John Hunter, they had come to regret the alliance and broke it off in 1745, forming their own Royal College in 1800. But even given the respectability of royal patronage, nothing was known of germs, for instance, or how they gave rise to

diseases. Germs were not identified until the 1860s, by a French professor, Louis Pasteur, and a German doctor, Robert Koch, working separately. Their discovery had infinite consequences. A Scottish surgeon, Joseph Lister, met Pasteur and wondered if these 'germs' were the cause of the deaths of so many patients after operations. In 1867 he carried out the first 'antiseptic' operation—on his own sister for breast cancer—and the value of scrupulously clean conditions was realized.

Many surgery patients also died from the pain and shock of the operation, for until the 1840s there were no anaesthetics other than alcohol. The inventor, Sir Humphry Davy, had discovered that 'laughing gas' (nitrous oxide) produced

►The head of an endoscope. A fibre brings in the light source (two bright dots) and the lens carries back the image. Because it is only 6 mm wide it can explore the body's highways to see what is wrong without necessarily having to resort to exploratory surgery.

Repairing Damage

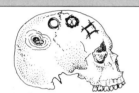

▲ 4 different trepaning methods —cutting holes in the skull to release evil spirits.

▲ 16th century Italian cosmetic surgery. Grafting skin from the patient's arm to replace skin lost from the nose.

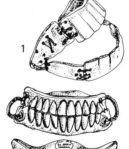

▲ Dentures: 1. Dentures on spring, Swiss, 1500. 2. Ivory dentures, 1810. 3. False teeth, 1880.

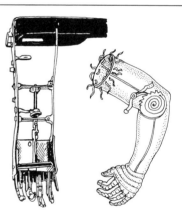

▲ Artificial arms: Early 16th c. iron hand (left). Late 16th c. French arm (right). A ratchet and pawl locked the elbow in any position.

▲ 2500 year old Hindu method of reconstructing a nose as described by Sushruta.

▲ Etruscan denture with gold bridgework, 700 BC.

Medical Machines

▲ Hippocratic bench, 400 BC— dangerous machine used to realign a dislocated thigh.

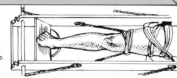

▲ Glossocomion, Rome AD 180. Galen's invention to reduce a fracture.

▲ Harvesting opium, an eastern anaesthetic for centuries (left) and Snow's ether inhaler, facepiece and drop bottle (right).

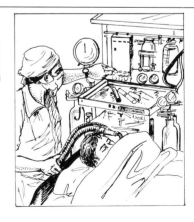

▲ Nadi-sveda, an Indian steam pipe to hasten the healing of a wound, 400 BC.

▲ Ether replaced rum as an anaesthetic (left) and in a Morton-Gould inhaler (right), 1847.

▲ At first anaesthetists administered their craft in street clothes.

▲ Since World War II surgery has become much safer. Here a trained anaesthetist monitors the flow of anaesthetic to the patient.

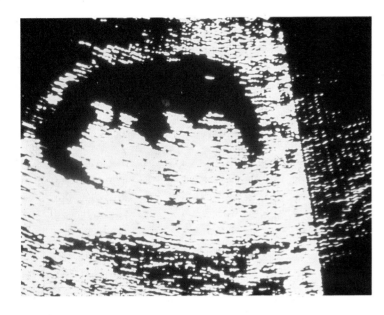

▲ An ultrasound scan showing the foetus in the mother's womb. The ultrasound machine sends out pulses of ultrasound that are reflected off the baby inside its mother. The echoes go to a machine that uses them to build up a picture of the baby on a screen. It is used to scan babies before they are born to see that their growth development is proceeding correctly and that they are lying in the right position for birth.

unconsciousness. An American dentist, Dr Riggs, persuaded another dentist, Dr Wells, to inhale the gas before having a tooth extracted. Dr Wells regained consciousness waving his arms delightedly and shouting, 'A new era in tooth-pulling!' It was soon found that ether was safer than laughing gas, and in 1846 an American surgeon used it for a serious operation. Later the same year it was successfully tried in London. 'Gentlemen,' said the surgeon, 'we are now going to try a Yankee dodge for making men insensible.' He proceeded to amputate the patient's leg in 26 seconds, without a murmur from the man.

Scientific research continued unceasingly. Sometimes years of patient experiment ended in disappointment, sometimes an accident brought a breakthrough. Chance, in this way, led to the discovery of X-rays in 1895 when Conrad Röntgen, a German physicist, because of the way that various pieces of apparatus were arranged on his work-bench, suddenly saw the bones of his own fingers shadowed on luminous paper. Röntgen's fame was now assured.

Similarly in 1928 Alexander Fleming saw that some mould on a culture plate by the window of his laboratory had destroyed a virus growth that he was studying. Even so, it was some years before its manufacture was developed. It took a Second World War, with all its suffering, to make the invaluable remedy, penicillin, available to all.

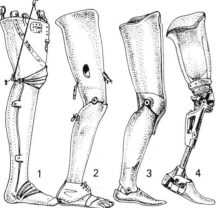

▲ Artificial arms: 16th c. iron hand with flexible fingers (left). Modern arm and hand (right).

▲ Artificial legs: 1. 16th c. French. 2. Belgian World War I leg. 3. Wooden leg. 4. Modern internal mechanism.

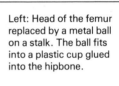

Left: Head of the femur replaced by a metal ball on a stalk. The ball fits into a plastic cup glued into the hipbone.

▲ Artificial heart made of silicone—still in the experimental stage.

▲ Ball and cage valve used to replace the diseased aortic valve in the heart.

▲ Modern cardiac pacemaker. The first model made in 1932 weighed 7.2 kg!

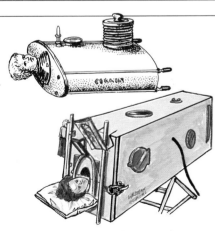

▲ Iron lung of 1876 (top) with a manual pump and of today (bottom). An iron lung takes over from the lungs when they fail.

▲ X-ray machine invented by Conrad Röntgen in 1895.

▲ Joseph Lister's carbolic acid sprayer was used as antiseptic during operations from 1875.

▲ Electrocardiograph, 1908. This instrument measures the electrical activity of the heart and is very useful in helping to diagnose heart defects.

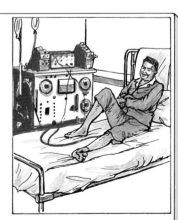

▲ Renal dialysis. This patient is attached to a kidney machine because his kidneys have failed.

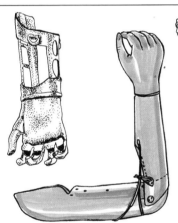

Hunters and Herdsmen

In a few corners of the earth there are people who still live by hunting, fishing or (where the climate is warm enough) gathering the nuts and berries that grow wild. Even so, they are not completely dependent on these foods as prehistoric man was, for usually they have some contact with civilization —they can trade fish or furs for flour, coffee and Coca Cola, or they may get help from a government agency.

Early Man had no such helpful neighbours. He was entirely on his own, dependent on his courage and cunning to track and trap his meat. The North American Indians continued this life right into the 19th century, hunting the huge herds of bison that grazed the prairie. All that ended when the white men built railways across the country, and the famous 'Buffalo Bill' (W. F. Cody) was hired to supply fresh meat to the workmen. In 18 months he shot 4820 bison. What with his efforts, and the farmers who took over the land as the railways extended, the vast hunting-grounds were soon no more.

Elsewhere and earlier in history the change had crept in slowly, over many generations. Something like 10,000 years ago it was realized that, since not all animals were as wild as others, some like sheep and goats could be caught and kept in pens, or even allowed to graze freely on the open hillside. A more intelligent animal, the dog, could actually be tamed and trained to keep the flocks and herds together.

This was a tremendous step forward. The life of a hunter had always been uncertain. Fish and meat could be dried and smoked to keep for some time, but future supplies could never be taken for granted. The herdsman, on the other hand, was sure of fresh meat wherever he went. He also quickly learnt to milk his animals, and then to make cheese. He had wool and goat's hair for clothing while the animals were still alive, and hides when they were killed.

The change to a 'pastoral' life had other effects. If the pasture was rich, people could stay in one place. Even if they had to move with the seasons, according to climate and water-supply, at least it was a regular yearly circuit. Now, too, they could own property—their flocks—and this could lead to trouble, as we have seen when discussing war. In most countries flocks and herds were in due course combined with crop-growing (see page 76).

◄ Horse wearing the correct tack for a gymkhana. The modern bridle developed very early as a method of steering the animal— Assyrian sculptures show horses with a length of rope looped round the horse's jaw. The earliest saddles were simply a folded blanket, but with the invention of the stirrup a method of attaching them had to be devised—the saddle was used as an anchor.

One important discovery, far back in time, was that male animals—bulls, rams, and stallions—could be made more docile by a simple operation on their sex organs, *castration* or *gelding*. Only a few males were needed—one ram would serve a whole flock of ewes to produce next season's lambs. No cattle-farmer wanted as many bulls as cows. So the excess of male calves were made bullocks and were either raised for beef or used to draw carts, as no bull would have done.

Most other changes in stock farming have come within the last 300 years. Before then, lack of winter feed meant that only a few breeding animals could be kept until the next year, and autumn saw a tremendous slaughtering and salting down of meat. But in 1724 English farmers began growing fields of turnips specially for the stock to eat when there was little grass. A great landowner, Viscount Townshend, pioneered this idea and was nicknamed 'Turnip' Townshend as a result.

Shortly afterwards, a 20-year-old Leicestershire farmer, Robert Bakewell, realised that sheep and cattle could be improved if the farmer mated only the best animals. He began his experiments in 1745, and his idea caught on as other farmers saw that carefully-bred stock produced more milk, meat and wool. Two centuries later came an elaboration of this development—artificial insemination—when it became unnecessary even to bring bull and cow together. The semen, or seed, of a pedigree bull hundreds of kilometres away could be implanted in cows to produce better calves on any number of farms. This process had been achieved with dogs by an Italian, Spallanzani, as long ago as 1779, but only in modern times has it been adapted to cattle-breeding.

Two simple everyday objects symbolize two other revolutions in farming: a can of meat and a strand of barbed wire. Canned meat began in 1812, long before can-openers had been devised. In 1840 the instructions on the label still advised the use of 'chisel and hammer'! The wide development of meat-canning made it worth raising huge herds, that could never have been marketed as freshly-killed meat. Those herds were raised particularly on the ranges of the United States and Argentina. On those vast open spaces the cattle on one ranch had somehow to be kept from straying elsewhere—and elaborate wooden fencing would have been impossibly expensive. Thin strands of cheap wire were twisted into barbs and marketed by an American, Joseph Glidden in 1874. It can be said that the Wild West was opened up not by the cowboys but by this cheap, nasty but invaluable invention that enabled farmers to spread their steers over acres of prairie land.

► Can of carrots and gravy taken on Sir Edmund Parry's Arctic exploration of 1824. Canning arose as a direct result of Napoleon's requirements for his troops during the Napoleonic wars. The first cans were glass jars with corks. The idea of a tin canister was introduced by Peter Durand, an Englishman. He sold the patent to Donkin and Hall who set up a canning factory. They supplied this can for the Arctic expedition.

CARROTS & GRAVY

Hunting Weapons

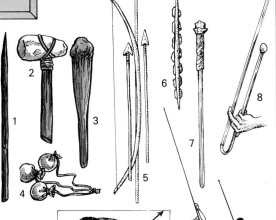

► Early hunting weapons: 1–4. The most complicated Stone Age weapons were the stone axe and the bolas (4). A bolas was made of 3 stones wrapped in animal hides and tied together with leather thongs. When thrown it wrapped itself around the legs of a running animal tripping it up. 5. 20,000 years ago hunters used a bow and arrow. 6. A slotted bone fish-spear, 8000 BC. 7. Wooden arrow, 8000 BC. 8. Spear thrower increases the length of the cast. A hook on the end fits into a hole at the end of the spear, 8000 BC.

▲ Egyptians using nets to trap wild duck.

▲ Mongol riders caught ponies with lassos on poles.

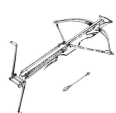

▲ Hunting in Africa with bow and arrow (left), and in South America with blow pipes (right) some as long as 5 metres (2000 BC–today).

▲ The Australian boomerang is thrown to kill. If it misses it returns to the thrower.

▲ Elaborate stone trap still used in France today.

▲ Hare hunt in ancient Greece, 400 BC. The Greeks used dogs to flush out the hares.

▲ Specially adapted crossbows were used to hunt deer in the 11th century.

▲ After the restrictions of the Commonwealth in 17th century England hunting was followed with great vigour. Otters were hunted particularly ferociously (left) using double pronged spears.

As a result the otter was hunted almost to extinction. Pheasant shooting was also popular although it looks odd to see hunters shooting on horseback (right).

► The most common hunting weapon used today is the shotgun which uses cartridges filled with shot. This particularly fine French model has two interchangeable barrels. The shotgun should be aimed just ahead of the target to allow for its movement. Shot pellets travel not in a lump but in a long line so even if the leading pellets miss those following will probably hit.

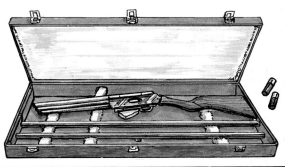

Animal Harnesses

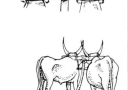

► The wooden yoke as a means of harnessing oxen has been in use for 5000 years. The most primitive yokes were only attached to the horns and centre pole by leather straps. Later a wooden bar was lashed under the ox's throat.

▲ In medieval times a wooden U-piece was added beneath the neck.

▲ This harness cuts into the horses' windpipes decreasing their efficiency.

▲ The Chinese realized the problem and designed a suitable harness but it was not capable of pulling heavy loads.

▲ Horses pull with the base of the neck —so this padded collar is designed to distribute the load around the shoulders. A bearing rein forces the horse to keep its head up.

► The whipple tree, first depicted in the Bayeux tapestry in the 11th century, allowed a load to be pulled round corners by three horses without putting all the strain on one horse.

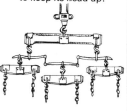

▲ 17th century coach. Traces connect the harness to the shaft. Notice how the horses' tails are pollarded to stop the hairs catching in the wheels.

Seed and Harvest

About the same time that men began herding animals they also started to gather the seed-grains of wild grasses to pound them into flour. It was happening in the Middle East by 9500 BC. It did not take people long to realize that there would be a bigger crop of such grains next time if they scattered some on the ground—and covered it so that the grains were not immediately devoured by the birds. The next step was to make some kind of implement that would break the surface of the soil. A sharpened stick or a deer-antler might be used, or a sharp flint could be fixed on the stick to make a hoe.

The invention of the plough was the great event in prehistoric farming. Drawn by oxen, it applied much more power. At first it merely gouged a deeper groove across the land. Then some nameless genius in Mesopotamia designed a plough that would also turn over the clods it cut through. This, and the shoulder-yoke to increase the pulling power of

the oxen, came in about 2000 BC. After that, except for the introduction of iron, there was no major change in the plough until the 18th century.

As with all things technical, the Romans were good farmers. They wrote books on agriculture and spread new techniques across their empire. They drained marshes, they lightened heavy clay soils with sand, and they knew the importance of manure as a fertilizer. But their system of slave-labour discouraged the invention of labour-saving devices. After all, what were slaves for if not to work? And the serfdom of the Middle Ages was no better—in Russia serfdom lasted until 1861 and as a result that country's farming was particularly backward.

In many ways farming stood still, with little change in tools or methods, until the so-called Agricultural Revolution which, like the Industrial Revolution, started in Britain.

A key date was 1701, when Jethro Tull designed his seed-drill, which allowed seeds to be sown economically in rows instead of being broadcast wastefully by hand. Later he invented a threshing machine and wrote a book, *Horse-Hoeing*

The Fields

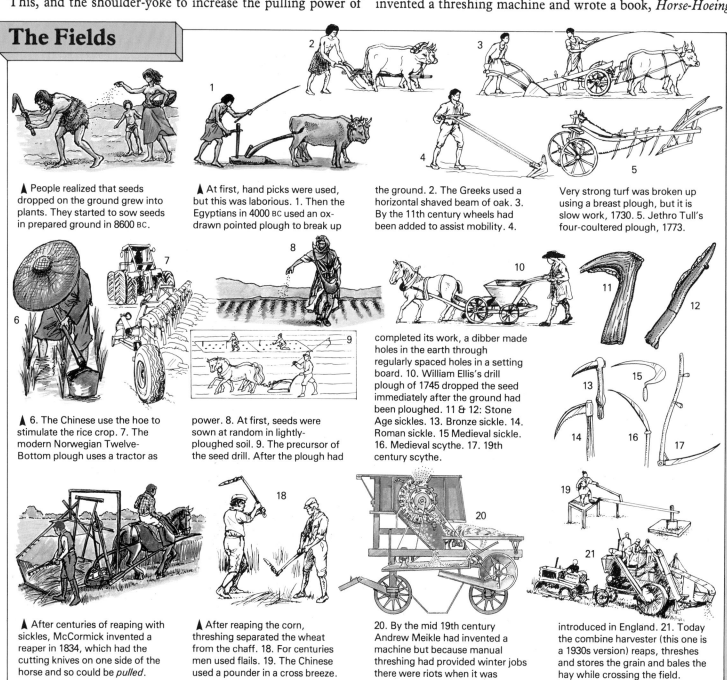

▲ People realized that seeds dropped on the ground grew into plants. They started to sow seeds in prepared ground in 8600 BC.

▲ At first, hand picks were used, but this was laborious. 1. Then the Egyptians in 4000 BC used an ox-drawn pointed plough to break up

the ground. 2. The Greeks used a horizontal shaved beam of oak. 3. By the 11th century wheels had been added to assist mobility. 4.

Very strong turf was broken up using a breast plough, but it is slow work, 1730. 5. Jethro Tull's four-coultered plough, 1773.

▲ 6. The Chinese use the hoe to stimulate the rice crop. 7. The modern Norwegian Twelve-Bottom plough uses a tractor as

power. 8. At first, seeds were sown at random in lightly-ploughed soil. 9. The precursor of the seed drill. After the plough had

completed its work, a dibber made holes in the earth through regularly spaced holes in a setting board. 10. William Ellis's drill plough of 1745 dropped the seed immediately after the ground had been ploughed. 11 & 12: Stone Age sickles. 13. Bronze sickle. 14. Roman sickle. 15 Medieval sickle. 16. Medieval scythe. 17. 19th century scythe.

▲ After centuries of reaping with sickles, McCormick invented a reaper in 1834, which had the cutting knives on one side of the horse and so could be *pulled*.

▲ After reaping the corn, threshing separated the wheat from the chaff. 18. For centuries men used flails. 19. The Chinese used a pounder in a cross breeze.

20. By the mid 19th century Andrew Meikle had invented a machine but because manual threshing had provided winter jobs there were riots when it was

introduced in England. 21. Today the combine harvester (this one is a 1930s version) reaps, threshes and stores the grain and bales the hay while crossing the field.

Husbandry. By this time Lord Townshend was persuading farmers to abandon another wasteful idea—instead of leaving each field idle, or fallow, once every three years, so that the soil could recover its lost goodness, they should adopt a 4-year rotation of wheat, turnips, barley and clover—each crop taking different nourishment from the soil and allowing the following year's crop to thrive. These men and others, like Thomas Coke, and the cattle-breeder, Bakewell, brought a new scientific spirit to farming, which spread first to North America, then to Germany, and later to other lands.

Since that beginning, new ideas and experiments have continued unceasingly for more than two centuries, with agricultural shows and societies and colleges founded to ensure that the knowledge spread quickly to the working farmers who would use it. Machines have been invented for every purpose. Chemists have concocted fertilizers and pesticides—not all of which have proved desirable. And just as Robert Bakewell showed the way to breeding better animals, scientists have shown that plants too can be bred to produce new varieties or richer yields. Here the pioneer was an

Austrian monk, Gregor Mendel, whose research on plant genetics began in 1858 but was not recognized as vitally important until 1900, long after his death.

Quite another kind of change followed the age of exploration (see page 69). The new continents of America and Australia took from Europe the farm animals that were unknown there, but in exchange they offered crops quite unfamiliar to the Europeans. The potato came over from America in 1573, though it was not widely grown or eaten for a long time. A few years later came the tomato from Mexico, but it too only gradually became popular, and was not eaten raw until the 19th century.

Modern farming is now a multi-billion pound specialist industry responsible for feeding the population of the earth: a bad grain crop in America and a large portion of the world starves. An idea of how specialized farming has become can be gleaned from these figures. In 1700, 90 per cent of the earth's population produced 100 per cent of the food required. Today only 3 per cent of the population produces 120 per cent of the food—the surplus is stored.

Milling

Above: Mill for crushing olives to make oil, 1500 BC. Windmill in Afghanistan with sails in the horizontal plane so no gears are needed (below).

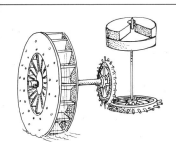

▲ Roman water-mill for grinding corn (above). Mediterranean windmill (below).

▲ Medieval windmill (above). Windmill with a fantail (right). The fantail was invented by a British engineer, Edmund Lee, in 1745. It turns the sails into the wind whenever the wind changes direction, so that the windmill works all the time that the wind is blowing. When the wind changes, the blades of the fantail begin to move which turns a set of gears that makes the cap of the windmill revolve. The sails move round until

they point into the wind, as a result the fantail blades stop turning and the cap comes to rest.

Irrigation

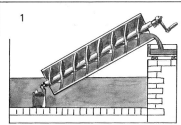

▲ Primitive irrigation—the *shaduf* (top), 5000 BC. The mill system (above) was built over a stream and the water flowed through culverts to the fields.

▲ Irrigating the Nile: 1. Archimedean screw. 2. The flood waters are held back in canals at the high water mark. The water was fed down through sluices.

▲ Chinese invented this chain pump to irrigate their lands from the Yellow River in the 2nd century BC.

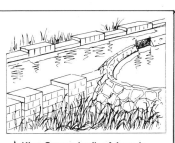

▲ King Sennacherib of Assyria built a system of canals which kept reservoirs filled for irrigation.

▲ Today's fields are irrigated by vast sprinkler systems that can supply water as a mist or at more than 2 cm an hour.

Materials, Methods and Men

Primitive people still make mud huts. But in Sumeria, by about 7000 BC, men knew that the hardest mud was dried clay, and that it was better to dry it in separate oblong lumps and then bind the oblong lumps into the wall they were building.

Even in the hot dry climate of the East these sun-dried bricks and tiles were not strong enough for all purposes. They could stand up to very light rainfall, but not to constant contact with water, as in drains and canals, so it was a great step forward when people learnt to harden bricks with fire, in 2000 BC.

The Romans brought bricks to northern Europe, but in Britain they went out of use. Stone was used in house-building if it could easily be quarried in the district, but mostly medieval houses were built using a frame of strong timbers carrying the weight of the roof. The spaces between the beams were filled in with anything that would keep out the weather—often sticks and twigs bound together with mud, known as 'wattle and daub', and plastered over, sometimes with beautiful decoration or 'pargetting'.

Castles and churches might have roofs of lead, but that was too expensive for lesser buildings. Slabs of stone or slate might be used, or chips of wood called shingles, but thatch was the most common, made of straw or reeds. Thatch, though, was a fire hazard, especially in crowded towns, where the flames spread from roof to roof and quite often a whole section of the town would be destroyed. So regulations were made to forbid thatch and discourage too much use of timber. As a result bricks and tiles came back into use from about 1200 onwards. At first they were imported from the Low Countries and bricks were sometimes referred to as 'Flanders tiles'. Later they were manufactured in England.

The brick was made to a standard size until in 1784 the government put a tax on them and the brickmakers simply used fewer and bigger ones. At this point bricks were made singly in hand-moulds—a good workman, with boys to help him, could make 5000 a day. They were then baked in coal-fired kilns, a cheaper and hotter fuel than wood. Then in response to the demand for more and more buildings to fill the growing cities, brick-making was mechanized by the invention of two machines. The first machine invented in 1825—the Lyle and Stainford Pugmill-Brickmaker—forced a soft wet clay into moulds. These were then baked in long 'clamps' a million at a time, sometimes for a month or more. The second machine, devised by Richard Bennett in 1879, extruded a stiffer mixture into a continuous rectangular sausage which was cut into bricks with wires. Breezeblocks, first made in Britain in 1932, are cheaper but less strong than ordinary brick and are composed of furnace ashes and cement.

Cement was needed to stick bricks and other materials together. The improved 'Portland' cement was invented by a Yorkshire bricklayer, Joseph Aspdin, in 1811, and kept a close secret until 1824. Cement, mixed with water, sand, broken stone, and other ingredients, produced concrete. It was first used in 1833 for a breakwater at Algiers, and the first concrete-mixer was used when building a bridge in Hungary in 1857. 'Reinforced' concrete, containing steel bars, was

Tools

▲ 1. Stone Axe, 400,000 years old. 2 and 3. Stone-bladed axe and pick, 6000 BC and 4500 BC (4.)

▲ 5. Using water to make wood swell splitting the rock. Pounding with hard stone. Chiselling.

▲ 6. Mason's drill, 2000 BC. 7. Roman plane in cast bronze. 8. Roman saw with bronze blade.

▲ 8. Medieval carpenter. 9. 3rd c. BC lathe—used for shaping wood by spinning it against a tool.

▲ Medieval tools. 10. Hammer. 11. Chisel. 12. Saw. 13. Pincers. 14. Knife. 15. Brace.

▲ 16 and 18. Box spanner and metal-worker's vice. 1676. 17. The screw—and screw-driver, 1676.

▲ 16th century rolling mill from Lorraine used to groove lead strips for window panes.

▲ Henry Maudsley's lathe, 1810 was first used to make accurate screws and replicas in quantity.

▲ Oxyacetylene welding was invented by Fouché and Picard in France, 1903.

▲ Lasers are used to cut metal. The laser produces a beam so bright it can be seen on the Moon.

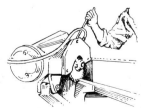

▲ Pneumatic drills use the power of compressed air to break up concrete.

▲ Circular saw for cutting *metal*. For heavy work the disc is cooled by jets of water.

introduced by Joseph Monier of Paris in 1867 and first used for a building in America in 1872.

'Prefabricated' concrete, in ready-made sections, was employed by a British architect, J. A. Brodie, to build a cottage in 1901 and then a block of flats in Liverpool in 1904. But the idea of prefabrication—building something with measured sections manufactured elsewhere—was not new. There had been the huge iron and glass Crystal Palace erected for the Great Exhibition in London in 1851, and, long before that, Nonesuch House brought over from Holland in 1578 and assembled on London Bridge. The idea was greatly developed after World War II, as a quick way to ease the housing shortage caused by bomb damage and growing population. The word 'prefab' was added to the English language. But sometimes the technique was applied too hastily to high-rise flats and similar schemes, and the results proved unsatisfactory—they fell down.

The building trade is one which calls for many different skills and men are classified accordingly as bricklayers, stonemasons, carpenters, plumbers, plasterers, and so on. In the Middle Ages they belonged to craft guilds, qualifying with a long apprenticeship, perhaps of seven years. Today, when we look at the sheer mass of, say, a medieval castle, or at the exquisite craftsmanship of a cathedral roof, we may wonder what sort of men did this work, all by hand, without power-tools or machinery. Were they down-trodden toilers, terrorized by lordly masters? Or simple pious fellows, working not so much for pay as for the glory of God?

Neither probably. They were not so unlike the trade unionists of today. In the 14th century, complaints were heard that stonemasons conspired together 'that no man of their craft shall take less on a day than they set'. It was alleged that they went in for restrictive practices—not working too hard so as to bring down the pay of their mates, and demarcation, refusing to do any job but stone-hewing or whatever. Though there was no tea the idea of the 'tea break' was strictly observed—the men working on York Minster in 1370 had their drinking-time guaranteed. We know the name of one such independent-minded workman at Cambridge in the 15th century—Robert Goodgroom would never pick up his tools again after the dinner-hour until he heard the clock 'smyte'.

▼ Making mud or clay bricks in Egypt. The method has changed very little in the past 5000 years. Each brick is formed in a mould and is then laid out in the sun to dry for a few days. Egyptian builders used a clay mortar to bond their bricks together. They were first-class bricklayers. The sizes of bricks varied over the centuries, and experts can use these variations to help date a building.

Lifting Devices

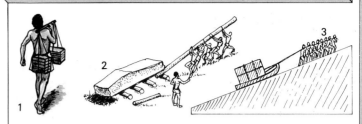

▲ 1. The earliest lifting device is a pole from which hangs the load allowing a double load to be carried. 2. Using a lever and rollers to manoeuvre a heavy stone into place. 3. A heavy block is dragged on a wooden sled along a wooden causeway. The runners of the sled are 'lubricated' with sand to make them run smoothly.

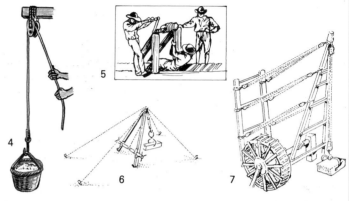

▲ 4. The pulley allows large weights to be hauled up vertically, 3000 BC. 5 and 6. The winch combines roller and lever to give continuous leverage, 600 BC. 7. Roman crane with human treadmill.

➤ Brunelleschi (1420) invented a special crane to build the lantern on top of Florence Cathedral. A frame enabled the builders to run a series of pulleys which moved the stone blocks laterally as well as vertically.

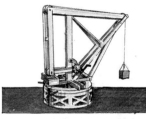

▲ Slewing jib crane designed by Leonardo da Vinci, 1490.

▲ Left: Hydraulic lift, 19th c. Right: Screw jack.

▲ A titan or travelling jib crane.

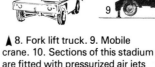

▲ 8. Fork lift truck. 9. Mobile crane. 10. Sections of this stadium are fitted with pressurized air jets which lift them 4 cm off the ground allowing sections to be moved around.

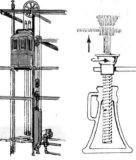

Projects and Plans

'Do-it-yourself' was the principle in early building. Even when simple shelters gave way to more elaborate houses, and individual men specialized in crafts, there was usually enough skill in the neighbourhood for everyday construction.

Vaster projects came with the growth of civilization. These required more imagination, more grasp of mathematics, and more organizing talent. The biggest Egyptian pyramid, built about 2575 BC, contains 6 million tonnes of stone—all of which had to be dragged to the site (there were no axles able to bear such weights) and laid in position without block and tackle or lifting gear of any kind. Yet the measurements are precise to within a few centimetres.

The earliest nation whose architecture has really influenced us down to this day is Greece. The ruins of the Parthenon, finished in 432 BC, still look down over Athens—and we see its general style, its long pillared frontage, imitated in countless city halls, museums, and other buildings.

But again it was the Romans who made the most progress. Their wealthy empire gave them the funds, they were great practical engineers—and they had mastered the use of concrete as well as brick and stone. They were not always as original as the Greeks (they were quite happy, usually, to imitate them), but they took over other people's ideas and made them work. The Greeks and earlier nations had known about the arch, but they did little about it: the Romans built superb arches and left their example to the world.

The Roman arch could span greater distances, using less

▼ Dome of Hagia Sophia, Istanbul built by Justinian in the 6th century AD, it is reputed to be the third largest unsupported dome in the world. Early domes were supported by continuous circular walls, which made them hard to build into square or rectangular buildings. Byzantine architects achieved this by raising the dome above the supporting walls on piers or *pendentives*.

Structures

▲ Red Indians made tents from a framework of birch poles covered with strips of bark.

▲ Suspension bridges of this type have been used for centuries to cross rivers in the Himalayas.

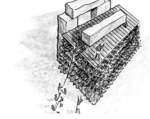

▲ The cross stones at Stonehenge were lifted on to increasingly higher platforms.

▲ Early example of a beam bridge made of granite on Dartmoor in Devon.

1. Egyptian arches were supported by an inner structure made of mud bricks sloped at a 45° angle to the wall. 2. Corbelled vault. Each course of blocks overhangs the course beneath. The projecting corners are smoothed off. 3. Gothic arch with the wooden centering used to build it. 4. Roman arch showing the centering and keystone. 5. Pantheon, Rome. 6. Circular dome supported by pendentives.

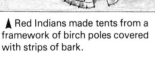

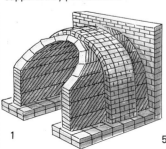

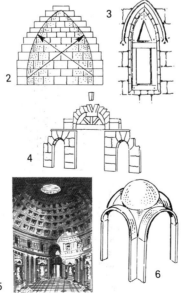

▲ Building a vault. Stones are laid along the wooden centerings. A specially shaped keystone is being hoisted up to complete the arch. When the mortar has hardened the centerings will be removed.

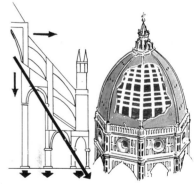

▲ Flying buttress (left) takes the main load of the building, walls could now be pierced with large windows. Dome of Florence cathedral showing the main ribs (right).

material than two posts supporting a lintel. In brick or stone an arch is built up of wedge-shaped pieces call *voussoirs*. They discovered that the weight of the arch tends to splay the feet outwards, so that the base of a single arch had to be very thick. On the other hand an arcade—a series of arches—need only be buttressed at each end. The Romans used this principle in aqueducts.

An arch that is extended backwards or forwards is called a vault. The Roman arched or *barrel* vault had the same problem as the arches—they had to be very thick at the base. The Romans realized that if they intersected two barrel vaults at right angles (called a *groin* vault) not only did it create more space but it needed buttressing only where the two vaults crossed. In the 13th century the Crusaders imported into Europe the Middle Eastern pointed arch. Builders found that the pointed arched vault allowed them to intersect two vaults of different widths. At about the same time church builders developed a way of transmitting the weight of a vault through arched struts, *flying buttresses*, to massive free-standing pillars outside the building. With this development the Roman arch finally became obsolete because now the walls no longer needed to be so thick and could be pierced with great stained glass windows and have delicate arcades.

The Romans also turned the dome into a major architectural feature and solved the old problem of thick walls by lightening the dome as much as possible. They used hollow brick ribs and further lightened it by gouging out square hollows or *coffers* from the interior surface of the dome.

In AD 112, the Romans built the Pantheon of brick and concrete. Until 1851 when the Crystal Palace was built its dome had the largest span in the world at 42.5 metres. It still stands as a monument to Roman civilization.

Classical Greek and Roman styles came back with the Renaissance. A book on architecture, by the great Roman Vitruvius, had been lost and forgotten for ages, until a copy turned up in a Swiss monastery in the 15th century. It opened men's eyes to new possibilities. An Italian, Palladio, went back to classical principles. A Welshman, Inigo Jones, toured Italy in 1603 and 1613, was entranced by the new 'palladian' buildings and introduced the style to Britain. Until then the designing was done by the master builder who was in charge of the day-to-day construction, the word architect being little used. Now began the modern division between planning and execution.

A new role for the architect came in the 17th century—to plan not just one grand building but a lay-out of small ones in terraces or squares or crescents. Some people think that town-planning is just a new-fangled modern idea. It is not. The Egyptians had new towns laid out on a geometrical pattern in 2000 BC. One of the first planners whose name we know was Hippodamus, born in Athens about 480 BC. Thirty years later he was commissioned to plan Piraeus, the port of Athens, and did so with wide, straight streets. His chessboard pattern was imitated afterwards at Alexandria. It is, of course, an obvious design for a city—it is found in the China of the Han emperors (200 BC onwards) and in Central America long before Columbus arrived. An improved version, with open spaces, was chosen by William Penn when he founded Philadelphia in 1682, and most North American cities were staked out on a grid pattern.

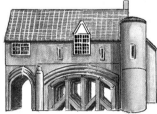

▲ The segmented arch with its centering is less than semi-circular in shape and was popular in the 15th c. The elliptical arch (right) is almost oval and is used for short bridges.

▲ If waterways need to be kept open during bridge building, then the bridge has to be built out from the banks. The arms are called *cantilevers*.

▲ Erecting the great arch of the Crystal Palace at Hyde Park in 1850.

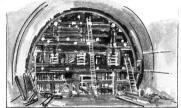

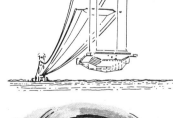

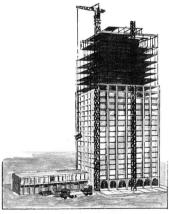

▲ Tower Bridge, London. Known as a bascule bridge, it operates on the principle of a drawbridge and is raised like a trap door. Tower Bridge was built in 1894 and it still stands today.

▲ Suspension bridges (top) are assembled section by suspended section, welded together to make a continuous box girder. The tunnel shield (above) protects workers boring through soft rock.

▲ 3 inventions made the skyscraper possible: steel girders, prestressed concrete and the safe hydraulic lift. Ready-made concrete and glass sections are lifted into place by tower cranes.

▲ The tallest monument in the world, the 192m wide stainless-steel parabolic arch called the Gateway to the West in St. Louis, Missouri. Eero Saarinen designed it in 1947. It was opened in 1966.

The Industrial Revolution

The word 'industry' makes us think of factories and ugly towns. This is not the whole picture, but it is the one that has been formed over the last two centuries.

It was not so, before. People who produced goods for sale were mainly craftsmen and apprentices in small workshops that were part of their master's house. In a few occupations men naturally worked in larger groups—in a stone-quarry, for instance, or a shipbuilding yard, but most trades could be carried on in small premises—even, in the case of spinning and weaving, in the worker's own cottage.

The exceptions were so rare that they became quite famous. John Winchcombe, known as Jack of Newbury, who died in 1520, was described as 'the most considerable clothier England ever beheld', because he owned 100 looms and employed 500 men.

What altered everything was the invention of power-driven machinery which brought large numbers together in one place to use it.

Until the 18th century power meant in most trades only man-power with occasionally a horse or bullock walking round in a circle driving a mill. The only other sources of power were watermills and windmills. Britain got its first watermills from the Romans, then their use was forgotten until the Anglo-Saxons introduced them again in the 8th century, and by the time William the Conqueror's Domesday survey was made there were nearly 6000. There were no windmills in Europe until about 1180, when the idea was brought in from Arabia where they had been invented, for in such a dry country the water-mill would have been useless.

Besides corn-grinding, watermills could be used for paper-making and 'fulling'—thumping cloth to cleanse and thicken it. And windmills could be used for draining water-logged land, which is why they became such a feature in Holland.

What we call 'the Industrial Revolution' still made considerable use of water-power but it was even more dependent on the development of the steam engine. Such an engine, piston-operated, was designed by Thomas Newcomen in 1712 and was used for pumping water out of mines. It was James Watt who went on to develop the invention to drive machinery in factories. In 1785 such a steam engine was installed in a spinning mill—and within another thirty years the cost of yarn had been reduced to one-tenth. Soon steam-power was taking over everywhere, and when George Stephenson adapted it to the railway locomotive (first train in 1825) there was soon a network of lines to carry raw materials and manufactured goods all over the country.

Making Cloth

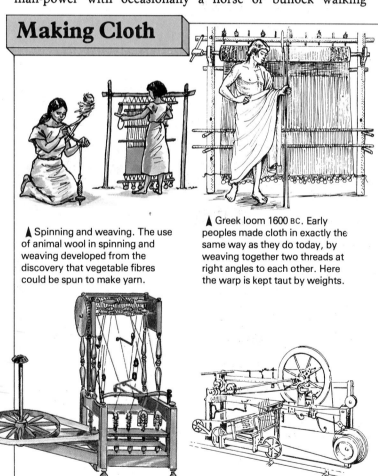

▲ Spinning and weaving. The use of animal wool in spinning and weaving developed from the discovery that vegetable fibres could be spun to make yarn.

▲ Greek loom 1600 BC. Early peoples made cloth in exactly the same way as they do today, by weaving together two threads at right angles to each other. Here the warp is kept taut by weights.

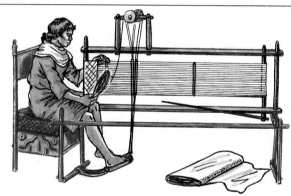

▲ The medieval frame loom had foot pedals to open the 'shed'—the alternative warp threads—so that the shuttle could be passed through. The pedals worked a special frame called a heddle.

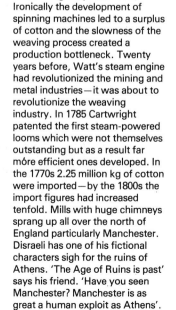

▲ Arkwright's spinning machine (above) called the water frame because it was powered by a waterwheel. The rollers spun the cotton at different speeds to make it fine and then wound it onto spindles to make it strong.

▲ Crompton's mule was invented in 1779 and called the mule because it was a cross between the jenny and the waterframe. It produced the finest thread on the market and was not replaced until 1828.

►Cartwright's power loom. Ironically the development of spinning machines led to a surplus of cotton and the slowness of the weaving process created a production bottleneck. Twenty years before, Watt's steam engine had revolutionized the mining and metal industries—it was about to revolutionize the weaving industry. In 1785 Cartwright patented the first steam-powered looms which were not themselves outstanding but as a result far more efficient ones developed. In the 1770s 2.25 million kg of cotton were imported—by the 1800s the import figures had increased tenfold. Mills with huge chimneys sprang up all over the north of England particularly Manchester. Disraeli has one of his fictional characters sigh for the ruins of Athens. 'The Age of Ruins is past' says his friend. 'Have you seen Manchester? Manchester is as great a human exploit as Athens'.

None of this would have been possible without plenty of iron. Iron had always been smelted with charcoal. As forests were cut down, this was not available, and Britain grew short of iron, which had to be imported. Then, in 1709, Abraham Darby found that coal could be turned into coke which was much better than charcoal. He established the first coke furnace at Coalbrookdale in Shropshire, which is regarded as the birth-place of the Industrial Revolution. His son used it to produce cast iron and his grandson supplied that iron for the building, in 1782, of the world's first all-iron bridge across the Severn—designed by John 'Iron-Mad' Wilkinson. The next great step was Bessemer's new process, in 1856, for making steel. Today about 700 million tonnes of steel are produced worldwide yearly and it is by far the most used engineering raw material. Steel was first made as early as 1000 BC by adding a measured amount of carbon to molten iron, but this remained a relatively minor activity until the 18th century when steel was in demand for instrument making; but the process was very laborious and was nearly 3000 years old. There is no question then that Bessemer's process and the open hearth process (see below) developed in 1864 dominated steel-making until the 1950s when the basic oxygen process superseded them.

These were the outstanding inventions that made Britain into the first industrialized country, 'the workshop of the world', with new collieries and mines starting everywhere,

▼ Raw viscose being prepared. Silk is very expensive and always has been. Hilaire Chardonnet in 1884 tried to imitate the process using chemicals and succeeded. In 1892 Charles Cross and E. J. Bevan devised the viscose process which was similar to Chardonnet's but used less flammable ingredients. Today viscose is second only to cotton in fabric manufacture.

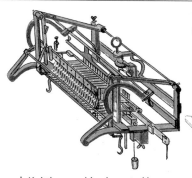

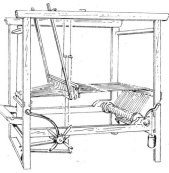

▲ Knitting machine invented by William Lee in 1589. It could knit at the surprisingly fast rate of 600 stitches every minute. It operated by treadle and pulley.

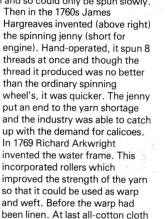

▲ The Hand loom 1733 (above left). By and large flax and wool were mostly used for weaving up until 1750. Then gradually cotton started to be used to produce calicoes. Before long the demand was greater than the supply. Weavers had a problem. The trouble was, the thread spun from the raw cotton was not strong enough and so could only be spun slowly.

Then in the 1760s James Hargreaves invented (above right) the spinning jenny (short for engine). Hand-operated, it spun 8 threads at once and though the thread it produced was no better than the ordinary spinning wheel's, it was quicker. The jenny put an end to the yarn shortage and the industry was able to catch up with the demand for calicoes. In 1769 Richard Arkwright invented the water frame. This incorporated rollers which improved the strength of the yarn so that it could be used as warp and weft. Before the warp had been linen. At last all-cotton cloth could be produced.

▲ The third factor in the cotton boom was Eli Whitney's cotton gin, (short for engine). His machine with teeth, brushes and rollers speeded up the process of separating cotton fibres from the seed.

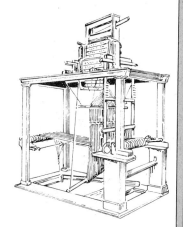

▲ Jacquard's loom, 1801, is a milestone in the history of weaving and a milestone in the history of automation. Perforated cards guide hooks to lift specific warp threads. They are still used for making patterned fabrics.

cotton-mills in Lancashire and woollen-mills in Yorkshire, blast-furnaces, foundries and factories turning quiet country places into noisy, smoke-hung, over-crowded towns. For the progress was by no means an unmixed blessing. It produced wealth for some and work for many, but it also produced appalling slum conditions and working hours, not only for men but for women and small children who today would be in a playschool. To remedy these evils long agitation was required to get laws through Pàrliament, and the organization of trade unions to extract better wages.

Britain started and led the Industrial Revolution. At the same time, before her own political revolution, France was still a land dominated by an out-of-date feudal system, and Russia far more so. Germany and Italy were not yet nations, but groups of separate little states. The American colonies were not yet independent and when they became so, in 1776, they were still occupied with developing their immense territory. Japan was closed to western ideas—power-driven factories were scarcely known until the 1870s.

So Britain had a flying start. After 1870, the other countries began to catch up, first Germany, then the United States. Even Japan had a highly developed industry by 1914. But the United States had taken first place, with a total production equal to that of Britain and Germany put together.

And many further changes were at hand—such far-reaching changes that, in the 20th century, we can speak of a Second Industrial Revolution.

There is no exact date when we can say that the first industrial revolution began to change its nature and become the second, though the first World War, 1914–1918, is a rough-and-ready milestone. The vital changes were of different kinds and spread over many years, so that the two revolutions overlap.

A cooper at work in Czechoslovakia. In countries with a wine industry or abundant forests the cooper's craft is relatively secure. However, where this is not the case the wooden barrel has been superseded by metal kegs which are more suitable for carrying liquid such as beer under pressure.

Inventing Power

Savery's **steam** engine of 1896 was used to pump water out of mine shafts. Steam from the boiler passed into a chamber which was then closed. Cold water from a spray condensed the steam creating a vacuum which sucked up the water discharging it into a tank outside the mine.

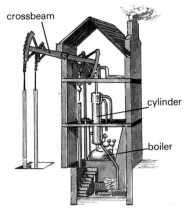

▲ Newcomen's engine of 1747 added a piston cylinder attached to a cross beam to the principle of Savery's engine.

▲ Faraday's disc dynamo, 1831.

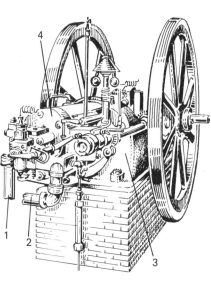

▲ Otto's engine of 1876 was the first successful internal combustion engine. It used a mixture of gas and air. Air (1) and gas (2) were drawn into the cylinder (3) by a piston (4). On the return stroke a burning gas jet outside the engine ignited the fuel mixture creating an explosion which produced the work stroke. Then the gases were forced out on the 4th stroke.

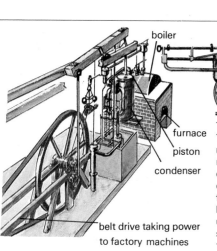

boiler

furnace

piston

condenser

belt drive taking power to factory machines

▲ Watt's engine of the 1780s added a separate condenser and a double acting piston for greater power and lower fuel consumption.

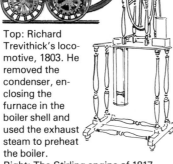

Top: Richard Trevithick's loco-motive, 1803. He removed the condenser, en-closing the furnace in the boiler shell and used the exhaust steam to preheat the boiler.
Right: The Stirling engine of 1817 did not use a boiler. The application of heat on to the outside of an air-filled cylinder caused the air to expand and then contract, powering a piston.

▲ Parson's steam turbines. Steam under pressure was released into a cylinder which turned a series of wheels with vanes, so fast that attached to a ship's propeller through gears they could drive a ship at up to 34 km/h.

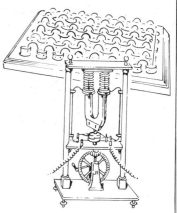

▲ Volta's pile (top) was the first source of **electricity** that had a continuous flow. By linking cups of salt solution with metal bows of silver and zinc, Volta created the first battery in 1800. Pixii's early generator, 1832 (above).

➤ Oersted had invented the electromagnet in 1820. Faraday discovered that a wire with an electric current passing through it suspended between magnets would spin round. He had created the electric motor. In 1831 he discovered that if a disc is rotated between magnets an electric current is produced—the dynamo, and with it the electrical industry, was born. The first attempt to apply Faraday's principle to a practical dynamo was made by Pixii in 1832. He arranged a horseshoe magnet that could be rotated with its two poles close to

two coils of wire. This hand powered machine produced a current. In 1881 this principle was harnessed on a large scale when Godalming in Surrey opened a power station that supplied electricity for the street lighting.

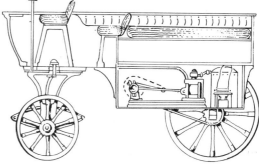

▲ The first **internal combustion engine** that worked was invented by Lenoir in 1860 and was powered by burning coal gas.

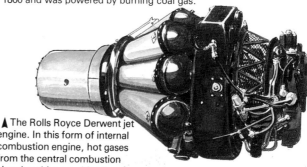

▲ The Rolls Royce Derwent jet engine. In this form of internal combustion engine, hot gases from the central combustion chamber drive a turbine to run a compressor, then emerge from the jet on the left.

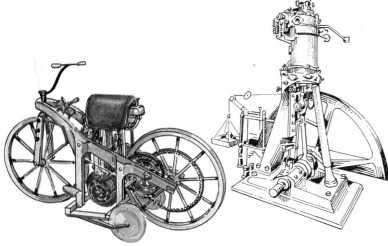

▲ The next step came when Daimler in 1883 improved the fuel mixture. Otto's engine had been connected to a gas main. Daimler created a portable engine by adding a carburettor to his engine which mixed petrol vapour and air to form an explosive mixture that was ignited by a spark. He attached it to a motorcycle in 1886. The rear wheels were driven by a leather band attached to the engine. The machine was so heavy that the rider had to lower two side wheels to support it when stationary.

▲ Rudolf Diesel made further improvements in 1892. Instead of detonating the fuel using a spark he used air heated by compression, thus removing the need for spark plugs. He used a cheaper fuel too. Early diesel engines had to be heavily built so at first they were used to generate electricity and as power units on ships. But work in the 1920s produced lighter diesel engines for use in cars. However for private cars diesel engines are less popular. They are noisier and size for size give less power.

▼ In 1942 Enrico Fermi built the first atomic 'pile' reactor. Inside the pile layers of granite alternate with uranium. The U-235 in the uranium gives off neutrons beginning a chain reaction. This energy can be harnessed for example to heat water, creating steam to drive turbines to produce elecricity. Unfortunately the knowledge which has enabled us to harness nuclear energy for constructive purposes has also been used to make bombs. Large sections of society are bitterly opposed to this.

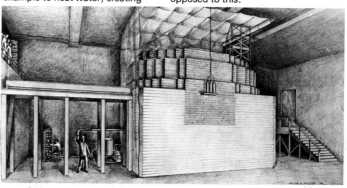

Mining

▲ Mining copper in Austria, 1200 BC.

▲ 16th c. lift pump used to drain mines of flood water.

▲ 17th c. European salt mine. The salt is cut out in blocks forming 'rooms' with pillars.

▲ English coal mine, 1790.

▲ Methane gas accumulated in coal mines and frequently exploded when ignited by the naked flame from a candle. In 1815 Davy invented the safety lamp which enclosed the light source in a lantern (left). The first American oil well, 1859 (centre). Oil Derrick, 1891 (right).

▲ The Anderton shearer carves coal out of the mine and transports it back to the surface on a conveyor belt.

▲ Giant grabs do the heavy work in open cast mines. Compare its size with the truck.

▲ Picks and shovels have been replaced by automatic diggers operated by remote control.

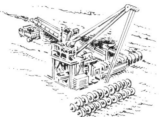

▲ Corkscrewing coal out of a thick seam above ground. This giant auger can bore up to 60 metres into the seam.

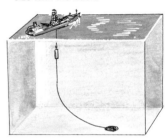

▲ Floating offshore oil platform. The five steel legs are lowered to anchor it to the sea bed ready for drilling.

▲ Extracting manganese from the deep ocean floor by vacuuming manganese nodules which lie loose.

During the first revolution industrial power became concentrated in leading European countries, the USA and Japan. They sold their manufactured goods to the rest of the world—much of it still dependent colonies in their various empires—and these less advanced territories produced raw materials in return. Their populations mostly had a low standard of life and, as they were in no position to bargain, they were exploited terribly by the industrial nations.

After two world wars, great revolutions in Russia and China, and countless struggles elsewhere, the old colonial empires began quickly to disintegrate into dozens of new independent countries, some huge like India (1947) and others very small. All were anxious to set up their own industries, which is what happened. Now industrialization has spread across the world, especially in the Far East, and with lower costs these countries can often outsell their older rivals. Once the cheap cottons of Lancashire were exported everywhere. Today, the Lancashire people more often than not will be buying the products of Taiwan or Hong Kong.

A second important change is that coal (the power source on which the first industrial revolution was based) has gradually lost its dominating position. Oil made a slow start. It was first drilled for in Germany in 1857, the first tanker was launched on the Tyne in 1863, and the first pipe-line (a mere 8 kilometres) was built in Pennsylvania in 1865. Its immense importance was not fully grasped until the arrival of fresh inventions, such as the internal combustion engine run on petrol.

Soon the demand for oil could not be met by the existing oilfields and there was eager competition to find new ones. The first under-sea oil was drilled, off the Californian coast, in 1900. In 1908 came the first commercial strike of oil in Iran, and soon the Near East developed into the main source. In 1973 the war between Israel and the Arab states interrupted the supply to the West, oil prices soared, and an economic crisis followed. Britain and Norway were lucky to find their own sources under the North Sea—the first of this oil came ashore in 1975 and by 1980 both countries had enough for their own needs.

Other sources of energy had developed earlier. The 19th century had brought gas and electricity. At first they needed coal to produce them, but nations lacking coal soon learned to harness waterfalls for hydroelectric power. And natural gas (used on a small scale as early as 1821 in America) was piped ashore in England from under the North Sea in 1967, and was enough to supply the whole of Britain.

But the earth's stores of 'fossil' fuels (coal, oil and natural gas) will not last for ever, so perhaps the most important development has been the peaceful use of nuclear power. Nuclear fission splits the atom and releases energy: such

Metals

▲ Copper and tin being smelted in a charcoal fire, 3000 BC. The bellows are used to raise the heat to separate the metal from its ore.

▲ Greek (top) and Roman (above) metalsmiths heating iron before hammering it into shape.

▲ Greek sculptor, 450 BC, making a bronze head by the lost wax method.

▲ 4 stages involved in making a cast bronze. (i) Wooden prototype to shape the mould. (ii) Mould. (iii) Sword in the mould. (iv) Sword.

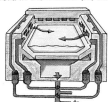

▲ Until the 18th c. the only means of smelting iron was with charcoal. When charcoal became expensive coke was used.

▲ Bessemer converter. Air was blasted through molten pig iron to remove the carbon. A quarter per cent was added to make steel.

▲ Siemens-Martin open-hearth process of making steel economizes on fuel and has been used to make most steel this century.

▲ The smithy (top) is centred round the open-hearth forge where the temperature is kept high with bellows. Blacksmiths made every metal artefact for agriculture, engineering and for the home. Above: French forge. The water wheel drives the giant forging hammer.

▲ Today huge ingots of iron are heated red hot and stamped roughly to shape in powerful hydraulic presses.

▲ When two pieces of metal need to be joined together a binding solder is used.

► The metal uranium has an unstable isotope Uranium 235 which is used in nuclear reactors to create energy to drive for example electric generators.

energy, when 'uncontrolled', produced the 1945 atomic bomb, but since 1951 it has also been 'controlled' in nuclear reactors for peaceful purposes. In 1952 the hydrogen bomb was devised from the similarly uncontrolled energy generated by nuclear *fusion* (the opposite process of welding together separate atoms to produce energy), and when this also can be controlled the world will have even vaster resources of energy for constructive purposes.

Besides the new sources of power, modern industry has been revolutionized by technological changes in every branch of production. In 1913 mass-production still called for thousands of workers to staff a factory. Today, robots and computers are quickly taking over much of the work. As early as 1928 a mechanical 'robot' opened a model engineering exhibition in London. In 1980 General Motors, in Detroit, introduced an industrial robot with electronic 'intelligence'—able to recognize different components on a conveyor-belt and choose which were needed.

Such inventions underline another great difference between the earlier industrial revolution and the one in which we are now living; the first meant more jobs for the growing population, the second means less. We have shortened working hours, lengthened holidays, cut out child-labour and enforced earlier retirement, but still have millions unemployed.

The changes we now need most are not technological but social—we need to hammer out new systems for sharing out the work more equally and sharing also the good things in life which it is within mankind's power to produce for all.

▲ A robot drilling a part presented to it in a specially designed jig at the Renault factory in France. Robots speed up the making of a car by a factor of 10. The first primitive robots introduced in America by Unimation in 1962 were of the 'pick and place' variety—they moved something from one place to another.

Living in Society

Learning to Behave

▼ Choristers from King's College, Cambridge. King's College School is a special choir school where only boys with exceptional voices are accepted. Of course, the boys are also taught normal subjects.

In the beginning men followed their tribal chief—he was often no more than a tough gang-leader—and as the ancient civilizations developed they had kings and emperors, handing on the power to their sons after them. The Greeks had kings at first, but *being* the Greeks, lively-minded and argumentative, they soon tried other forms of government. Besides monarchy (one-man rule) and aristocracy (rule by the 'best' people) and oligarchy (rule by 'the few') they were the first, in the 5th century BC, to invent democracy, rule by the *whole* people, dropping their votes into urns to be counted.

Even then it was not strictly the 'whole' people who ruled a Greek state like Athens. There were no votes for women, or slaves, or aliens born elsewhere. But at least all free-born Athenian males were equal, and the population was small enough for them all to attend the big open-air assembly, speak and vote on all the matters for decision. It was well over 2000 years before any country got as near as that to genuine democracy.

Governments, in whatever form, rule according to the laws they create. We may grumble at rules, but most of us soon find out, at school, that we like to be clear just what we may do and what we may not. Rules, too, protect us from other people's unfair behaviour and allow us to get on with our own lives unmolested. Men long ago discovered this. The 'rule of law' is the basis for true civilization.

In Paris, in the Louvre, we can still see the black stone monument set up by King Hammurabi of Babylon about 1790 BC. On it is inscribed his list of laws—and they were not the earliest laws, just a clearer rearrangement of them.

Of all ancient peoples the Romans have had most influence upon our legal system today. Their code was based on the Twelve Tables, a list of laws adopted in 450 BC, though many went further back. The Romans had a gift for drafting good clear laws, as they had for building good straight roads. They used juries, as the Greeks had done, and magistrates of different kinds to pass sentence.

Both the Greeks and the Romans allowed experts to argue the case (like our professional lawyers today) on behalf of ordinary people who could not speak well or did not know the law. We can still read some of their court speeches, especially those of the Greek Demosthenes (384–322 BC) and the Roman Cicero (106–43 BC). Demosthenes was born into a rich family. Unfortunately for him he was swindled out of most of his money. Compelled to earn a living he became a professional speech writer for contestants in law suits. Soon he was appearing in court on his contestant's behalf. By the time he died Demosthenes was the greatest orator of the age. In 322 he took poison to avoid capture when Athens was taken by Antipater and Craterus.

By the time of the Roman emperor, Justinian (AD 483–565), the laws had been accumulating for over 1000 years and no one could remember them all. Justinian had them all sorted out and embodied in a simpler, more consistent 'Code' which became the basis for many European systems centuries later.

A completely different system, Islamic law, came in about a hundred years after Justinian. This is based on the Koran, put together after Muhammad's death in 632. And it remains the basis of law in the Middle Eastern countries.

From early times the kings have had to listen to their councils of powerful lords and bishops. Gradually this evolved into a parliament—a place to *parle* (speak). This idea started in England.

For centuries Parliament met only occasionally and was very limited in its powers. But slowly the idea grew that the King ought to govern according to the wishes of his people. Charles I would not accept this. Civil war broke out in 1642. He was defeated by the armies of Parliament under Oliver Cromwell, and executed in 1649 as a traitor to his own country. In 1688 his younger son, James II, clashed with his people again and was driven off the throne in 'the Glorious Revolution'. Since then, every British monarch has accepted that the real power rests with the parliament elected by the people.

Unfortunately not all countries have attempted to follow this democratic course. All Communist states, for instance, and some others as well, allow only one party. Going to vote is a formality, since the result is a foregone conclusion. There is no way of changing the government.

▼ A contrast in disciplinary methods. Left: Ringe State prison, Denmark where inmates are allowed to live together. Right: San Quentin Gas Chamber, United States.

Schools

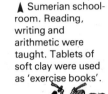

▲ In primitive societies education was concerned with passing on techniques for survival.

▲ Sumerian schoolroom. Reading, writing and arithmetic were taught. Tablets of soft clay were used as 'exercise books'.

▲ Greek teachers teaching boys the alphabet which begins *alpha, beta*.

▲ Aztec *telpochcalli* schools teach boys how to fight.

➤ In medieval times the only schools were monastery schools. The monks taught reading, sums, literature and botany.

➤ A lecture at Bologna University, one of the oldest universities in Europe.

▲ An Elizabethan schoolroom.

▲ Prayers at a Church School, 1860.

◄ After Lord Shaftesbury's Factory Act, children had time for school. Many were built. Run by a board of managers they were called Board Schools.

▲ Education is regarded as an investment in the future. Countries need skilled people to help the country to develop.

▲ The relaxed atmosphere of a modern primary school contrasts with the stern discipline of the Tudor schoolroom.

Punishment

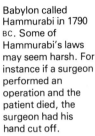

▲ One of the first law codes was conceived by an Amorite king of

Babylon called Hammurabi in 1790 BC. Some of Hammurabi's laws may seem harsh. For instance if a surgeon performed an operation and the patient died, the surgeon had his hand cut off.

For minor theft culprits were held in the stocks (left) or the pillory (right). Culprits in the pillory had rotten fruit thrown at them.

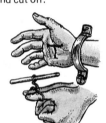

▲ Women wore a scold's bridle for nagging, and men a barrel for being drunk.

▲ Thieves were branded. The thumbscrew was used to extract a plea.

▲ The ducking stool (left) was used to punish nagging women. Trial by Ordeal (right): a man had to pick a stone out of boiling water. If his hand blistered he was guilty.

◄ Far left: Iron Maiden. When the doors were closed the victim was impaled. Near left: Breaking on the wheel was carried out by the executioner. Each limb was smashed twice with an iron bar before a blow to the heart brought death. Above left: The rack was used by the Spanish Inquisition to extract confessions. It was used in England from 1447 until 1628 when it was banned.

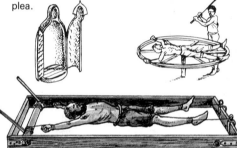

▲ Until quite recently people were condemned to death for committing even quite small crimes. Death was often by hanging. Forgery and counterfeiting were never considered as petty crimes, for they were regarded as a direct attack on the monetary system and property of the nation. When paper money came into use, the notes sometimes carried the severe warning 'Death to forgers'.

▲ Charles I was tried by Parliament, found guilty as a tyrant and sentenced to death despite much opposition. He was executed at Whitehall and impressed everyone by his dignity.

Left: A prison treadmill. In Victorian times, crimes were tried according to the law which by now was very sophisticated and much fairer than in previous centuries. During the French Revolution of 1879 anybody who opposed revolutionaries was liable to be guillotined (above). The guillotine was recommended by Dr Guillotin who was a kindly man, horrified at the way most executions were botched. It is ironic that the name of this gentle person has come to symbolize the excesses of the Terror.

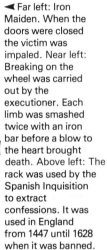

Money Matters

'You can't manage without money,' people warn us, and they are right—in our modern world. Yet for almost the whole of humanity's long history men *had* to manage without money, for it was not invented. What they could not produce themselves they had to get by exchange with others.

This barter system can be very awkward. Try buying a railway-ticket with a surplus hamster. Yet somehow the ancient civilizations contrived, for centuries, to trade goods and pay taxes without currency. Gradually, though, bright-minded individuals in various countries saw how much better it would be to agree on some handy, portable token that would help A to sell his produce to B and then buy something else from X or Y or Z.

The Aztecs of ancient Mexico decided to use little cocoa beans, which were so bitter that nobody had thought of turning them into chocolate. The Celts used iron bars. The cowrie shells found in the Indian Ocean provided a convenient currency in much of Asia and Africa.

Metal proved the most practical. It was durable and, if it was rare, a small piece was valuable. Gold was best of all, for it was lightest to carry and did not rust or tarnish. Asia had gold, but the Greeks did not have enough to make into money, so they used silver. In ancient Italy there was copper, so the first coins there were made of bronze. Assyria, in about 700 BC, had coins of lead. Many Greek silver coins, nearly as old, have survived to this day, often punched with beautiful designs.

Although coinage spread widely over the world it was still not used for all purposes. Peasants, for instance, paid their rents and Church dues in 'kind', that is to say, actual produce, carrying their corn to be stored in a tithe barn. Lords at first paid the King for their lands by providing him with soldiers. But the use of money grew steadily, and Henry V paid his troops by borrowing from wealthy merchants like Dick Whittington.

Merchants by then were becoming very powerful. They had agents and customers in far-off cities—Florence and Genoa, Bruges and Augsburg. When they settled accounts they had

▼ Inside the big GUM department store in Moscow are many galleries. The shopstalls are tucked away under the arches so that people can stroll freely along the central passageways.

Money

▲ Early forms of money took many strange shapes. 1. and 2. Chinese, AD 100. 3. Moroccan tree money. A piece could be broken off and given as change.

▲ In early societies people did not use money. They exchanged goods or *bartered*. Here Indians are bartering furs for food.

▲ 'Cash' circulated in China from AD 618 to 1910.

▲ Top: Gold stater, Carthage. Above: Indian sea shells were used as money.

▲ Our word bank comes from the Italian word *banca* meaning 'bench'. The early Italian bankers set up their stalls or benches in the market and dealt with their customers on the open street. People brought their money to the banker's strong room for security. The banker gave a receipt for this money which the customer presented when he wanted his money back.

Shops

▲ The Greek market place was called the agora and was the town's main meeting place. People from surrounding villages would bring wares to sell.

▲ Chinese market, AD 100. The man in the drum tower sounds the time when business must close for the day.

▲ Above: In a 13th c. market town tally sticks (top) were used as receipts. The stick was split between the 2 people.

▲ Aztec market place. Anybody caught stealing is tried before this special court. In the background a sentenced thief is being beaten to death.

no need to send sacks of money to and fro along the dangerous roads. It could be done by signing papers. In the same way, travellers could carry letters of credit and draw cash wherever they went.

When it came to sending a ship across the world on a trading voyage that might last a year or longer, few merchants could have afforded the expense—especially since they would not get a penny back until the ship returned. So they had partners to share the cost and the profit they hoped for. The first English 'joint-stock company' was the Muscovy Company which traded with Russia—240 merchants combined to raise the capital of £6000. Similar companies were formed by several countries to trade with different parts of the world. The East India Company, formed in London in 1599, led eventually to India's coming under British rule. The Hudson's Bay Company (founded in 1670 and still in business) played a great part in the development of Canada.

This was an important period in the history of money. Goldsmiths—who had strong vaults and guards for their own precious goods—were often asked to take care of their customers' valuables or to lend cash on their security. In 1633 a goldsmith named Lawrence Hoare became the first to accept cash on deposit. He was thus the first banker in England. But Amsterdam had had a bank since 1609 and Hamburg since 1619. It was a Stockholm bank which in 1661 issued the first bank notes. England had no paper money until the Bank of England was founded in 1694. The first English cheque still in existence was for £10 and dated 22 April 1659. Cheques were hand-written entirely until 1763, when Hoare's Bank supplied them in printed form.

Nowadays the whole banking system is so closely linked that

Engraving of 1813 of the Royal Mint on Tower Hill, London. Mints are places where coins are manufactured, usually with the authority of the state.

countless transactions can be made without actual money changing hands. Credit cards (introduced by the Diners' Club of New York in 1950) enable people to sign for goods and services they want. If they do need cash, however, they can have another type of card which, slipped into a dispenser in the outside wall of a bank, will enable them to draw money at any time, day or night.

We are assured that by the end of this century people will be doing their shopping electronically from their own armchairs —studying the various offers on the screen and merely pressing keys to order what they want.

Perhaps, like prehistoric man, we *shall* be able to 'manage without money'. It could be wonderfully convenient—but it could also be terribly dull.

Top: Oldest existing Bank of England note issued on 19 December, 1699 for £555. Above: Because of the terrible inflation in Germany in 1928, this 1 billion mark note would have bought less than 1 mark today.

This army token can only be spent in army shops.

Left: The money changer in a middle eastern market conducts his business in similar surroundings to his ancestors. His work is made easier by a modern calculator. Above: The first credit card for general buying was issued in 1950 by Diners' Club. The credit card has reduced the role of cash in our society to the extent that many people carry no cash at all.

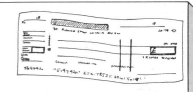
Above: Although banks issue their customers with cheque books in which to write orders for the amount of cash they want to pay someone else, cheques can legally be written on anything. To prove this the writer A. P. Herbert presented a cheque written on a cow. The bank accepted it and paid him the money.

Butcher's shop, 1790. In 1790 veal and pork were 3½d per lb and a hind quarter of lamb 4½d per lb. Meat was eaten in enormous quantities too.

Victorian costermonger. Originally a seller of costards (a large apple) it came to mean a man who sells food from a barrow.

Billingsgate fish market in Victorian times. Fish were being sold at Billingsgate close to London Bridge from the 12th c.

The first supermarket was opened by Michael Cullen in New York in 1930. By 1932 he had 8 stores and a turnover of $6 million.

Index

Abacus *64*
Aborigine *8, 24, 58*
Acting *41*
Acupuncture *70,* 71
Africa *53, 69, 75*
Agriculture 74, 76–77, *76–77*
Aircraft 18–19, *18–19*
Alarm clock *66*
Alcohol *49*
Alexander the Great 22, 24, 67
Alexandria 9
Algebra *64*
Alphabet 10, 11, *89*
Aluminium 55, 59
American Indians *48, 50, 70, 74, 80, 90*
American War of Independence 25
America's Cup *17*
Anaesthetic *72, 72*
Analytical Engine *64*
Angle measurement *66, 68*
Animal classification 67
Animal harness *75*
Animal sport *38–39*
Antiseptics *72, 73*
Apothecary *70, 72*
Aqueduct *62,* 81
Arabs *9, 22, 23, 28, 44, 64, 65, 67, 70, 86*
Arch 80, *80, 81*
Archimedes 60
Archimedes screw *9, 77*
Architecture 81
Arctic exploration *74*
Aristophanes 41
Aristotle 65
Arkwright, Richard *82, 83*
Arm, artificial *72, 73*
Armchair *56, 57*
Armour 26, *26–27*
Army 24, *26, 91*
Artificial insemination 74
Artificial limbs *72, 73*
Artillery *24–25*
Assyrians *9, 26, 32,* 42, *56, 77*
Astrolabe *16*
Astronomy *9,* 64
Athens 41, *88*
Atlantic crossing *17*
Atom 67, 86
Atomic bomb 87
Atomic clock 67
Automation *86, 87*
Automobile *see* Motor car
Axe 46, *75, 78*

Babbage, Charles *64*
Babylonians *9, 14, 64,* 88, *89*
Backgammon 37
Bacon, Francis 67
Bagpipes 42
Ball-games 38, *38–39*
Ballistic Missile Early Warning System *see* BMEWS
Balloon 18
Ball-point pen *11*
Banking *90,* 91
Banknote *8, 89, 91, 91*
Barbarians *9, 22,* 25
Barbed wire 74
Barometer *66*
Baseball 39, *39*
Basket-making 46
Bassoon *43*
Bass viol *42*
Bastille *23*
Bath *63*
Bathroom 62–63, *62–63*
Battery *85*
Bay window *54*
Bear baiting *39*
Bed 56, *56–57*
Bell, Alexander Graham *16*
Bellows *87*
Bennett, Richard 78
Benz, Karl 15
Berthelot, Gilles *27*
Bessemer converter *87*
Bessemer steel 83
Bible *45*
Bidet *62*
Billiards 37
Billingsgate market *91*
Binary *65*
Binocular microscope *68*
Biplane *18*
Biro, Josef *11*
Blacksmith *87*
Blériot, Louis 19

Blitzkrieg *27*
Blood 71
Board-games 36, 37
Board Schools *89*
Boat *8, 16,* 17
Bodice 34, *35*
Bologna University *89*
Bomber *18, 19*
Book *10,* 11, *89*
Boomerang *75*
Boot 33, *33*
Botany 67
Bow and arrow 25, *75*
Bowls *38,* 39
Boxing 38, *39*
Bramah's closet *63*
Brandy *49*
Brassière 34, *35*
Brass musical instruments 43, *43*
Bread 58
Breezeblock 78
Brick 78, *79, 80,* 81
Bridge *80, 81,* 83
Bridle *74*
Bronze *56, 87,* 90
Bronze tools *76, 78*
Brownie camera *47*
Brummell, Beau *29*
Brunel, Isambard Kingdom *16*
Buffalo Bill 74
Bugle *43*
Building 50, 78, *79,* 80
Buoy *16*
Burial *49*

Cabinetmaker 46
Cable-laying ship *16*
Caesium atomic clock *67*
Calculator 64, *64–65, 91*
Caliper *66*
Calotype process *47*
Camera *47*
Camera obscura *47*
Camp bed *56, 57*
Canal 77
Candle 55
Canning *8, 74, 74*
Cannon 24, 25, 26
Canoe *16*
Can-opener *8*
Cantilever *81*
Cards 36, *37*
Carpentry 78
Carpet sweeper *61*
Carriage 14, *15*
Cartridge *25*
Cartwright's power loom *82*
Cash register *65*
Castle 26, *26, 27, 52, 52,* 56, 59, *63,* 78, 79
Castration 74
Catapult *24*
Cathedral 79, *80*
Cattle-farming 14, 74
Cave painting 44
Celts *14, 24, 50,* 90
Cement 78
Central heating 57
Chain-mail *see* Mail
Chair *56–57*
Chandelier 55
Chartres Cathedral *54*
Chemise 34
Chemistry *9,* 67
Cheque 91, *91*
Chimney 57, *60*
Chinese civilization *9, 10, 11, 12, 14, 17, 31, 35, 40, 48, 51, 53, 55, 56, 64, 66, 70,* 71, *75, 76, 77, 81, 90*
Chippendale settee *57*
Chocolate 48
Chronometer *67*
Church building *79, 80,* 81
Church music 42
Church School *89*
Circulation of blood 71
Circumnavigation 69
Circus *42–43*
Cittern *42, 43*
Civil War, English 88
Clarinet 43, *43*
Classification 67
Clay tablet 10, *10, 89*
Clipper ship *16,* 17
Clock *66–67*
Clog *32,* 33
Cloth *28, 29, 31, 34, 82, 82, 83*
Clothing 28–33, *28–33*
Clown *32*
Coach 14, *14, 75*
Coal 57, *83, 86, 86*
Cocoa 48, 90
Cocoon 31
Code of law 88, *89*

Cody, W. F. 74
Coffee 48
Coinage *8, 90, 91*
Coke *87*
Coke furnace 83
Colonial empires 86
Colt revolver *25*
Columbus, Christopher 9, 69
Combine harvester *76*
Commedia dell'Arte 41, 43
Communism 88
Compass 17
Composing machine *11*
Compound microscope *68*
Computer *64,* 65, *65,* 87
Computer games 37
Concorde *19*
Concrete 78, *80,* 81
Conveyor belt *86*
Convoy *27*
Cook, Captain *67,* 69
Cook, Thomas 21, *21*
Cooking *58,* 59
Copper *86, 87,* 90
Corn-grinding *77,* 82
Corset *35*
Cosmetic surgery *72*
Cotton 31, *82, 83,* 84, 86
Cotton gin 83
Counterfeiting *89*
Courts 88, *90*
Cow 74
Cradle *57*
Crane *79*
Crecy, battle of *24,* 25
Credit card 91, *91*
Cricket 38, *39,* 49
Crime *89*
Crinoline *29*
Crompton's mule 82
Cromwell, Oliver 88
Crop rotation 77
Crops 76
Crossbow *24,* 25, *75*
Crystal Palace 79, *81, 81*
Crystal radio *12*
Cuba 69
Cuban crisis 23
Cubism *45*
Cubit *66*
Curfew *61*
Cutlery *58,* 59
Cutty Sark 16, 17
Cylinder lock *53*

Da Gama, Vasco 69
Dagger *25, 71*
Daimler, Gottlieb 15, *85*
Dali, Salvador *35*
Dampier, William 69
Dance *43*
Darby, Abraham 83
da Vinci, Leonardo 18, *44, 79*
Davis Cup 39
Davy, Humphry 72
Davy's safety lamp *86*
Decimal system 64, 65
Decoration 46, *60*
Delacroix, Eugène *45*
Democracy 88
Democritus 67
Demosthenes 88
Dentistry *72, 73*
Derby *9*
Diesel engine *85*
Digger, automatic *86*
Directoire fashion *32, 33*
Discus *39*
Disease 71, *72*
Dish washer *61,* 62
Dissection 71
Doctor *57, 70, 71,* 72
Dog *49, 58,* 59, *74, 74*
Doll *36,* 37
Dome *80,* 81
Door 52, *53,* 54
Double bass *42*
Double glazing *54*
Doulton's water closet *63*
Drainpipe 50, *62, 62*
Drama 41
Draughts 36
Drawbridge *26, 52*
Dress *see* Fashion
Drill *71, 78, 87*
Drilling rig *86*
Drink *49, 49*
Drugs 71
Drum *42*
Ducking stool *89*
Dye *29,* 31
Dynamo *84*

Earring 34
Earthenware *63, 63*

East India Company *91*
Edison, Thomas 55
Education 37, *88, 89*
Egyptians *8, 9, 16, 20,* 24, *26,* 31, *32, 44, 46, 48, 49, 50, 53, 56, 58, 62,* 64, *64, 66,* 69, *70,* 71, *75, 76, 79, 80, 80,* 81
Eleanor of Aquitaine 29
Electric calculator *65*
Electric cooker *58*
Electric fire *61*
Electricity *85,* 86
Electric motor *85*
Electric train *36*
Electrocardiograph *73*
Electromagnet *85*
Electronic machinery 65, *65, 68, 87, 91*
Electronic music *43*
Electronic toys 37
Elizabeth I of England 28, *28*
Ellis, William *76*
Ellis, William Webb 38
Endoscope *72*
Energy 50, *82–84, 82–85,* 86
Engine *see* Machinery
English housing *51, 53,* 54
ENIAC (Electronic Numerical Integrator and Calculator) *65*
Eratosthenes 64
Ether *72,* 73
Euclid *64*
Euripedes 41
Execution *89, 90*
Exploration 22, 69
Eye make-up *35*

Face powder *35*
Factory *15,* 31, 46, 57, *82,* 84, *87, 87*
Factory Act *89*
Falconry *49*
False teeth *72*
Fantail windmill *77*
Faraday, Michael *84, 85*
Farming 74, 76–77, *76–77*
Farthingale *28*
Fashion 28–33, *28–33,* 34
Fermi, Enrico *85*
Field-gun *25*
Fields *76, 77*
Film-making *47*
Fire-arms *25*
Fireplace *57, 60,* 61
Fishing *49*
Fission 86
Flail *76*
Flapper *29, 35*
Flax 31, *83*
Fleming, Alexander 73
Flight 18–19, *18–19*
Florence cathedral *79,* 80
Flour mill 60, *60*
Flushing *63*
Flying boat *18*
Flying buttress *80,* 81
Food 59, 77
Foot-binding *33*
Football 34, 38, *38*
Foot soldier 25, *25*
Footwear 33
Forceps *67*
Ford, Henry 15, *15*
Forge *87*
Forgery *89*
Fork *58*
Fortification *25,* 26, *26–27*
Fossil fuels 86
Fouché 78
Fountain pen *11*
Four-poster bed 56
French Revolution *23, 89*
French window *54*
Fresco 44, *44*
Frying pan *59*
Furniture *56–57*
Fusion *86*

Galen *71, 72*
Galileo *66, 68*
Galoshes 33
Games 36–37, *36–37*
Ganges river *31*
Gardening 50
Garrick, David *41*
Garter belt *35*
Gas lighting 55
Gas oven *58*
Gazette *12,* 13
Geiger counter *66*
Generator 50, *85*
Geometry *64*
Geyser *63, 63*
Gin 49, *49*
Giotto 44, *45*
Gladiator *38,* 71

Glass 46, 54, 55
Glider *18*
Globe theatre *40*
Gold *32,* 90, *90*
Goldsmith 91
Golf 39
Gondola *20*
Gothic arch *80*
Grain 76, 77
Grand National *39*
Grand Tour 21
Great Bed of Ware *56*
Great Eastern steamship *16*
Great Wall of China 26
Great Western (liner) 17
Greeks *9,* 21, 24, *26,* 36, *36, 38, 38,* 40, 41, 44, *45,* 49, *51, 53, 62, 64, 64,* 67, 69, *70,* 71, *71, 75, 76,* 80, 81, *82, 87,* 88, *89, 90, 90*
Guilds 46, *52,* 72, 79
Guillotine *89*
Gunpowder *24,* 25, *25*
Gutenberg, Johann *10,* 11
Gymkhana *74*
Gymnastics *39*

Hair-style *32, 32–33*
Hammurabi, Babylonian King 88, *89*
Hand loom *83*
Hand weapons *24–25,* 25, 46
Hanging *89*
Hargreaves, James *83*
Harp *42*
Harpsichord *43*
Harrier aircraft *19*
Harrison, John *67*
Harvey, William 71
Hat *28–29,* 32, *32–33*
Hauberk *26, 27*
Haydn *43*
Headgear 32, *32–33*
Healing *70, 71, 72*
Hearth 56, *57,* 59
Heating *51,* 60–61
Heinkel, Ernst 19
Helicopter *19*
Helmet *26, 26, 27*
Henry the Navigator 69
Herbal medicine *70*
Herodotus 21
Hindenburg airship *18*
Hip-bath *63*
Hippocrates 71
Hockey 38, *38,* 39
Hooke, Robert *68*
Horse 14, *74, 75, 76*
Horse-racing 38, *39*
Hosiery *28,* 34
Hotel *21*
House-numbering 52
Housing 50, 52, *50–53,* 54, 56, *60,* 78, 80
Hudson's Bay Company *91*
Hughes, Howard *18*
Hunter, John *72*
Hunting *8, 38, 39,* 74, *75*
Hydraulic lift *79, 81*
Hydroelectric power 86
Hydrofoil *16*
Hydrogen bomb 87
Hygiene *72*
Hypodermic syringe *71*

Ice hockey 39
Impressionism *44*
Incas *9, 64*
India *20, 31, 35,* 41, *48,* 64, *64,* 72, *86, 91*
Industrial Revolution 8, *82–83, 82–83,* 87
Insulation *51, 54*
Internal combustion engine 15, 18, *84, 85,* 86
Iron *83, 87*
Iron Age 26
Ironing *30*
Iron lung *73*
Iron Maiden *89*
Islam *23,* 28, 44
Islamic law 88

Jack *79*
Jacquard's loom *83*
Japan *35, 40, 48, 54, 84,* 86
Jazz 43
Jenny, spinning *83*
Jet engine 19, *85*
Jewellery 34, *35*
Jig, mechanical *87*
Jones, Inigo 81
Journalism 13
Jousting *39*
Jury 88

Keep *26, 27*

Key *53*
Keystone *80*
Kidney machine *73*
Kindergarten 37
Kinetoscope *47*
Kitchen *58, 59, 59*
Kitchen utensils *58, 59, 59*
Kite 36
Knickers 34
Knife *58, 59, 78*
Knitting machine *83*
Knossos *44, 62, 62*
Knot (nautical) *66, 85*
Koran 44, 88

Lace *29, 33*
Lamp *55*
Lancashire 86
Lancet *71*
Laser *78*
Lathe *46, 78*
Latrine *62, 63*
Lavatory *63, 62–63*
Law 88, *89*
Lawn mower *9, 60*
Lawn tennis *39, 39*
Leaded window *54, 54, 78*
Lead soldiers 37
Leather 33
Leeuwenhoek microscope *68*
Leg, artificial *73*
Legion *24, 26*
Lenoir, Étienne 15
Letterbox *52*
Lifting devices *79, 80, 81, 86*
Light meter *66*
Linen 31
Lister, Joseph *72, 73*
Lock *53*
Locomotive *82, 85*
Locomotive, toy *36, 82*
Logarithms *64*
Longbow *24, 25, 26*
Loom *30, 31, 60, 82, 83*
Lord's cricket ground 39
Lost wax method *87*
Lumière brothers *47*
Lute *42, 43*

Machine-gun *25, 25*
Magellan, Ferdinand 69
Magistrate 88
Magnetic compass 17
Maiden Castle *26*
Mail *26, 27*
Make-up *34, 34, 35*
Manganese *86*
Mangle *30*
Marconi, Guglielmo *12*
Marco Polo *17, 69*
Marie Antoinette 29
Mass production *15, 15, 31, 46, 87*
Mathematics *9, 64, 65*
Mayas *9, 38, 48, 64*
MCC (Marylebone Cricket Club) 39
Measurement *64, 65, 66*
Meat *74, 91*
Medicine 70, *71–73, 72–73*
Mesopotamia 9, 10, 76
Metals *87, 90*
Methane gas *86*
Microcomputer *65*
Micrometer *66*
Microscope *68, 69*
Microwave oven *58*
Midwifery *70*
Milk 74
Mill *30, 31, 60, 60, 82*
Mining 82, 83, *84*, 86–87, *86–87*
Mini-skirt *29*
Minoan civilization *35, 44, 62*
Mint *91*
Mirror *35*
Missile 24, 25, *27*
Model T Ford *15*
Monastery 21, *56, 63, 70, 89*
Monet, Claude *44*
Money 89, 90–91, *90–91*
Monopoly 37
Montezuma *20*
Montgolfier brothers 18
Moog synthesizer *43*
Morris, William *46*
Morse, Samuel *12*
Mosquito net *53, 57*
Motor car 15, *15, 20*
Motorcycle *15, 85*
Movable type *10*, 11
Movie camera *47*
Mud brick *78, 79, 80*
Mud housing *50, 51, 52, 78*
Mule, spinning *82*

Music 42–43, *42–43*
Musket 25, *25*
Muslims 23, 28, 32, 49

Napier, John *64*, 65
Natural gas 86
Navigation *16*, 17
Necklace 34, *35*
Needle *30*
Neoclassicism *45*
Neolithic people *35*, 46
Net *53, 57, 75*
Newcomen, Thomas 82, *84*
News *12*, 13
Newspaper *10, 11, 12*, 13
Newton, Isaac 65, *68*
Nicotine 49
Niépce, Joseph *47*
Nightingale, Florence 70
Non-stick pan 59, *59*
North Sea oil 86
Nuclear energy *65*, 86
Nuclear reactor *87*
Nuclear warfare 23, *24*
Numeration 10, 64, *64–65*
Nursing *70*
Nylon 34

Oak *51, 56*
Oersted, Hans Christian *85*
Oil 86, *86*
Oil derrick 86
Oil painting 44
Olive oil *77*
Olympic games 38, *38*
Omnibus 14
Open-cast mining 86
Open hearth process 83, *87*
Operating theatre 70, *72, 72, 73*
Opium *72*
Opthalmoscope *71*
Orchestra 42, *43*
Organ 42, 43, *43*
Otto's engine *84, 85*
Oughtred, William *64*, 65
Oven *58*
Owens, Jesse *39*
Ox *75, 76, 76*
Oxyacetylene welding *78*

Pacemaker *73*
Package-holiday 21
Painting 44, *44–45*
Panama hat *32*
Pankhurst, Emily *9*
Pan pipes 42
Pantheon *80*, 81
Pantomime *40*
Paper 10, *10*
Paper-making *82*
Paper money 8, *89, 91, 91*
Papyrus 10
Paraffin heater *63*
Paraffin lamp *55*
Parchment 10
Park, Mungo 69
Parliament 88
Parry, Edmund *74*
Parson's steam turbine *85*
Parthenon *80*
Pascal, Blaise *64*
Passport 21
Pasteur, Louis 72
Pathé movie camera *47*
Pearl Harbor *22*, 23
Pelota *39*
Pen 10, *11*
Pencil *11*
Penicillin 8, *73*
Penny Post *52*
Permanent waving 32
Perspective 44
Pets *48, 49*
Petticoat 34
Phalanx 24, *26*
Photography *47*
Photostatic copying *11*
Phototypesetting 13
Physician see Doctor
Piano 43, *43*
Picasso, Pablo *45*
Pillory *89*
Pillow *56*
Pipe, musical 42
Pipe, tobacco *48*
Pitched roof 50
Plague *70*
Plane *78*
Plastics *59, 63*
Plastic surgery *71*
Plate armour 26, *27*
Plate glass *54, 55*
Plato *41*, 67
Playing cards *37*
Plough 14, 76, *76*

Plumbing 62
Pneumatic drill *78*
Pocket watch *67*
Poetry 38
Police *27*
Polynesia 35
Pompeii 54
Pony Express *12*
Pop music 43
Popular press 13
Portcullis 26, 52, *52*
Postal service *12*
Potato 48, *25*
Pottery 46, *46*
Power station 85
Press *10*, 13
Pressure cooker *61*
Prestressed concrete *81*
Printing *10*, 11, *11*
Prison *88, 89*
Projectiles 24–25
Projector *47*
Propeller 17
Protractor *66*
Pulley *60, 79*
Punishment *88, 89, 90*
Pyramid 80

Quadrant *16*
Quant, Mary *29*
Quartz crystal watch *67*
Quill *11*

Rack *89*
Radar station *27*
Radiator *61*
Radio *12*
Railway *15, 15, 20, 82, 85*
Ramparts 26, *26*
Rattle *36, 37*
Reactor *85, 87*
Reaping *76*
Recorder *43*
Reeds 10, *16, 17, 50, 50, 54*
Refrigerator *61*
Reinforced concrete 78
Religious drama *40*
Religious education *89*
Religious warfare 23
Renaissance 11, *54, 81*
Revolution 8, *86, 88, 89*
Revolver *25*
Rice *76*
Rifle 25
Riot gear *27*
Roads 14
Robot *87, 87*
Rocket 25, *25*
Rolls-Royce *20*
Rolls Royce jet engine *85*
Röntgen, Conrad *6, 73, 73*
Roof 50, *78, 79*
Rotary press *10*
Rowing 17
Royal Mail coach *14*
Rubber 33
Rugby football 38

Saddle *74*
Sailing ship 8, *16*, 17
Samurai 26
Sandal *32*
Sandglass *66*
Sash window *54, 55*
Saw *71, 78*
Scalpel *71*
School 88, *89*
Scissors *30*
Scold's bridle *89*
Screw-driver *78*
Screw jack *79*
Screw-propeller 17
Sculpture 44
Sedan chair *14, 20*
Seed-drill 76
Semaphore telegraph *12*
Servant *56, 57, 59, 63*
Sewer 63
Sewing machine *30, 31, 31, 61*
Sex appeal 28
Sextant *16*
Shaduf *77*
Sheep 74
Shells *90, 90*
Sheraton furniture 57
Shield 26, *26, 27*
Ship *16, 85*
Shoe 33, *32–33*
Shops *90–91*
Shotgun *75*
Shower *62, 63*

Silk 28, 29, 31, *32, 33*
Skin graft 72
Skull *71, 72*
Skyscraper *81*
Slave *58, 76, 88*
Sledge 14, *14, 79*
Slide rule *64, 65*
Smith, Adam 72
Smoking *48, 49*
Soap *62*
Socrates 65
Solar heating *61*
Soldier 25, *25*
Soldier, toy *36, 37*
Space travel 19
Spanish Inquisition *89*
Spinning 31, 82, *82*
Spinning wheel *30, 31, 60*
Spit *58, 59*
Sport 34, 38–39, *38–39*
Sprinkler *77*
Stagecraft *40, 41*
Stage make-up *35*
Stained glass 54, *81*
Stainless steel 59
Staircase *52, 56*
Steam engine 13, 15, 31, *61, 82, 82, 84, 85*
Steamship *16*, 17
Steel 83, *87*
Stephenson, George 82
Stethoscope *71*
Stiletto heel *33*
Stirling engine *85*
Stirrup 8, *25, 74*
Stockings see Hosiery
Stocks *89*
Stockton and Darlington railway 15
Stone Age 8, *24, 55, 75, 76, 78*
Stonehenge *80*
Stringed instruments 42, *42*
Sugar 48, *49*
Sumerians 9, 10, *26, 53, 54, 60, 62, 64, 71, 78, 89*
Sundial *66*
Supermarket *91*
Supersonic aircraft 19
Surgery 70, 71, *71, 72, 73*
Surrealist movement *45*
Surveying *66, 68*
Suspension bridge *80, 81*
Swimming *39*
Sword 24, *25*
Symphony 43
Synagogue 32
Synthetic material 34

Talbot, Fox *47*
Tally stick *90*
Tank 25, *27*
Tarot cards 37
Tattooing 35
Tea 48
Teddy bear *36, 37*
Telegraph *12*, 13
Telephone *12*
Telescope *68*
Television *12*
Telex *12*
Tennis *39, 39*
Tent *50, 80*
Thatch *50, 78*
Theatre *40, 41*
Theft *89, 90*
Theodolite *68*
Threshing 76, *76*
Thumbscrew *89*
Tiles *51, 78*
Times, The *11*, 13
Tin *87*
Tinned food see Canning
Tithe barn 90
Toaster *58*
Tobacco *48, 49*
Tomato *77*
Tools *71, 78*
Toothbrush 63
Toothpaste 63
Torricelli, Evangelista *66*
Toupée *32*
Tourniquet *71*
Tower Bridge *81*
Town crier *12*
Town-planning 81
Toys *36–37, 36*
Track events *38–39*
Trade 48, *65, 67, 82, 90*
Trade unions 84
Train, toy *36, 37*
Tram *15*
Transport 14–15, *14–15, 20, 21*
Trapeze act *42*
Travel 14–15, *14–15, 16, 17, 20, 21*
Travel agent 21

Treadmill *58, 59, 79, 89*
Trench-warfare *25*
Trepaning *72*
Trevithick, Richard 15, *85*
Tsai-Lun 10
Tuba *43*
Turbine *85*
Turbo train *15*
Turkey 48
Turnip 74
Turnspit 59, *60*
Type, printing *10*, 13
Typewriter *11*

Ultrasound scan *73*
Underground railway *15*
Underwater photography *47*
Underwear 34, *35*
United Nations Building 55
United States see America
University *89*

Vaccine *71*
Vacuum cleaner *61*
Vault *80, 81*
Venetian painting *44*
Vertical take-off warplane *19*
Vespucci, Amerigo 69
Vice *78*
Video camera *47*
Villa *51*
Viol *42*
Viola *42*
Viola da Gamba see Bass viol
Violin *42, 42*
Violoncello *42*
Virginal *43*
Viscose *83*
Vodka 49
Volta's pile *85*
Vote *9*, 88

Wages 57
Waggon 14, *14*
Waltz 43
War correspondent 13
Warfare 22–23, *22–23, 26, 26–27*
Warp *82, 83*
Warplane 18, 19, *19*
Washing 63, *62–63*
Washing clothes *30, 31*
Wash stand *62*
Wastepipe *50, 63*
Watch *35*
Water-carrier 62
Water clock *66*
Water-closet 63, *63*
Water frame *82, 83*
Water-heater 63
Waterloo, battle of *12*
Water-mill *77, 82*
Water pipe 48
Water wheel *87*
Watt, James 82, *82, 85*
Wattle and daub 78
Weapons 24–25, *24–25, 75*
Weather forecasting 66
Weaving 39, 41, 46, 82, *82, 83*
Welding *78*
Wheel 14, *14, 76*
Wheelbarrow 14
Whisky 49
Whist 36
White face make-up 34, *34, 35, 43*
Whittle, Frank 19
Wig 33, *33*
Wimbledon championships *39, 39*
Wimple 28, *32*
Wind instruments 43
Windmill *77, 82*
Window 54, *54, 55, 78, 80*
Wine 49
Witch doctor *70*
Woman's rights *9*, 88
Wood 50, *50, 51, 52, 52, 53, 57, 62, 78, 78, 84*
Wooden leg *73*
Woodwind instruments 43
Wool 74, *83, 84*
Wrestling *38*
Wright brothers 18, 19
Wrist watch *67*
Writing 10, *10*

Yacht *17*
Yale, Linus *53*
Yoke *75, 76*

Zeppelin 19
Zero *64, 65*